The Journal of the History of Philosophy Monograph Series
Edited by Richard H. Popkin and Richard A. Watson

The Philosophical Orations of Thomas Reid

DELIVERED AT
GRADUATION CEREMONIES IN
KING'S COLLEGE, ABERDEEN,
1753, 1756, 1759, 1762

Edited with Introduction and Bibliography by
D. D. Todd

Translated from the Latin by
Shirley Darcus Sullivan

Published for
The Journal of the History of Philosophy, Inc.

SOUTHERN ILLINOIS UNIVERSITY PRESS
Carbondale and Edwardsville

92   91   90   89   4   3   2   1

Library of Congress Cataloging-in-Publication Data

Reid, Thomas, 1710–1796.
The philosophical orations of Thomas Reid : delivered at
graduation ceremonies in King's College, Aberdeen, 1753, 1756, 1759,
1762 / edited with introduction and bibliography by D. D. Todd;
translated from the Latin by Shirley Darcus Sullivan.
p. cm.—(The Journal of the history of philosophy monograph series)
"Published for the Journal of the History of Philosophy, Inc."
Bibliography: p.
1. Philosophy—Early works to 1800.   I. Todd, D. D.   II. Title.
III. Series.
B1532.A5 1989
192—dc19   88–21133
ISBN 0–8093–1468–1   CIP

CONTENTS

For Joanne, Jonathan, and Aaron,
with gratitude for the liberality of their love and
the generosity of their forbearance.

THE *JOURNAL OF THE HISTORY OF PHILOSOPHY*
Monograph Series

THE *JOURNAL OF THE HISTORY OF PHILOSOPHY* MONOGRAPH SERIES CON-sisting of volumes averaging 80 to 120 pages, accommodates serious studies in the history of philosophy that are between article length and standard book size. Editors of learned journals have usually been able to publish such studies only by truncating them or by publishing them in sections. In this series, the *Journal of the History of Philosophy* presents, in volumes published by Southern Illinois University Press, such works in their entirety

The historical range of the *Journal of the History of Philosophy* Mono-graph series is the same as that of the *Journal* itself—from ancient Greek philosophy to the twentieth century. The series includes extended studies on given philosophers, ideas, and concepts; analyses of texts and contro-versies; new translations and commentaries on them; and new documentary findings about various thinkers and events in the history of philosophy.

The editors of the Monograph Series, the directors of the *Journal of the History of Philosophy,* and other qualified scholars evaluate submitted manuscripts.

We believe that a series of studies of this size and format fulfills a genuine need of scholars in the history of philosophy.

Richard H. Popkin
Richard A. Watson
—Editors

Introduction[1]

THOMAS REID WAS BORN AT STRACHAN, IN KINCARDINESHIRE, ABOUT twenty miles from Aberdeen, on April 26, 1710 (Old Style), exactly one year to the day before Hume. Like that of his contemporary, Immanuel Kant, Reid's life wholly lacked dramatic incident; he suffered no exile because of political disfavor, as had Locke, nor did he sail against foreign coasts as a member of a military expedition, as Hume did, or journey to the wilds of America to convert savages to Christianity as Berkeley did. Reid received his early education in Kincardineshire and then entered Marischal College, Aberdeen, in 1722 at the age of twelve. He received his B.A. degree in 1726. Thereafter he studied theology and was licensed as a minister in the Presbyterian Church in September, 1731. He served as Librarian of Marischal College from 1733 to 1736, and from 1737 to 1751 he served as pastor in the church at New-Machar. It was while living at New-Machar that he began studying Hume's *Treatise of Human Nature* (1739).

Reid was appointed regent and, later, professor of philosophy in King's College, Aberdeen, in 1751, replacing Alexander Rait, regent, who had died a few days before Reid's appointment. His connection with King's College lasted until May 1764 when he succeeded Adam Smith in the professorship of moral philosophy in the University of Glasgow. Reid published his first book, the *Inquiry into the Human Mind on the Principles of Common Sense* in the same year. He held this post until he died on October 7, 1796, at the age of eighty-six.

---

1. Editorial footnotes are indicated by numerical superscriptions. The translator's notes are indicated by asterisks. Reference to Reid's published works are to *The Philosophical Works of Thomas Reid,* ed. Sir William Hamilton, 8th ed., Edinburgh, 1895, available in a reprint published by George Olms, Hildeshiem, 1967. This edition of Reid's works is printed with two colummns to the page. Hereafter, "a" will indicate the left-hand colummn and "b" the right-hand column of a page in this edition. Thus H 300a refers to the left-hand column of page 300 of Hamilton's edition of 1895.

In 1780, Reid ceased active teaching and delegated his teaching duties to an assistant, but he remained in the university as a lively participant in philosophical discussions. Most of his remaining time, however, was spent writing the *Essays on the Intellectual Powers of Man* (1785) and the *Essays on the Active Powers of Man* (1788) and overseeing their publication. Both these books were worked up from voluminous lecture notes that Reid had prepared and collected for many years. His only other philosophical writings published in his lifetime, apart from the *Inquiry*, were an *Essay on Quantity* that had appeared in the *Transactions of the Royal Society* for 1748 and *A Brief Account of Aristotle's Logic*, written in 1767–68 and published in 1774 in the second volume of Lord Kames's *Sketches of the History of Man*. His *Statistical Account of the University of Glasgow* was apparently written in 1794 and was published posthumously in 1799 in the twenty-first volume of the *Statistical Account of Scotland*.

Reid was the chief figure in a group of philosophers who constituted the Scottish school of common sense. Historically, Reid has the best claim to be the originator of the "philosophy of common sense" even though earlier philosophers adumbrated it in sundry ways; Reid, anyway, synthesized diverse philosophical ideas, his own and others', to produce the philosophy of common sense.

Why should Thomas Reid be of interest to anyone but historians of philosophy? Part of the answer has to do with the intrinsic interest Reid's philosophizing has for contemporary philosophers who are familiar with it. But apart from them, Reid ought also to be of interest to educated laymen because of the extent of his influence on American political, literary, and philosophical culture. Thomas Jefferson, for example, was personally acquainted with Dugald Stewart, Reid's best disciple and explicator, and was converted by him to the common sense philosophy of Reid and his school. Jefferson considered the Scottish philosophy to be a sound basis for the sort of liberal democratic education he hoped the University of Virginia and other academies would provide, and he sought the assistance of Stewart in recruiting teachers from Europe. Indeed, it was precisely through the enormous influence of Scottish philosophy on American education that Reid's influence was exerted. For the first fifty years or so of the American republic, if any philosophy at all was taught in any American academy it was generally the Scottish philosophy, and the texts were the works of Reid and Stewart or texts derived directly from them. The first twelve or so academic generations of postrevolutionary American youth were steeped in the thought of Reid and his associates. Jurists, authors, and scientists all were imbued with what was widely regarded as the only sane, down-to-earth philosophy worthy of an American. Such thinkers as Emerson and

Thoreau were deeply indebted to Reid in their early years before they wandered off into the mists and bogs of New England transcendentalism. Even after Reidianism ceased to be orthodoxy Reid's influence continued. Charles Sanders Peirce, for example, praises Reid highly and claims him as a direct philosophical ancestor; at one point Peirce even named his own philosophy "critical commonsensism." By the time William James and, somewhat later, John Dewey flourished, Reid's influence had waned in America, as it had earlier in Britain in consequence of the combined assaults of Kantians, Hegelians, and Utilitarians—an odd alliance if ever there was one. Even so, traces of characteristic Scottish doctrines are to be found in both James and Dewey, particularly in their insistence on the continuity of science with common sense and their doctrine that reason and nature can never be in fundamental conflict in the ways Hume thinks they are. Reid's influence on American philosophy is still being felt. Noam Chomsky, to mention perhaps the most notable example, acknowledges Reid as one of his most important precursors.

Undoubtedly, however, it is largely for their influence in shaping American fiction that Reid and Scottish philosophy are of interest to nonphilosophers. As Terence Martin has argued so persuasively, the dominant position of Scottish philosophy in American education shaped early postrevolutionary fiction by inculcating a strong distrust of the imaginative depiction of social reality in fiction.[2] Under the sway of the common sense philosophy, Americans came to prefer their realities straight and without any fancy or fabricated trimmings. The result was that American writers wanting to write fiction were turned toward romance. In the romance, the imagination was liberated from the constraints of experience and "reality" and won a certain legitimacy for itself that the Scottish philosophy appeared not to allow. With an ever increasing mastery of the materials of the free fictive imagination, American literature flowered in Hawthorne, Poe, and Melville. Paradoxically, in constraining the literary imagination, the Scottish philosophy liberated it. American authors and their readers thus owe a considerable but little-known and unacknowledged debt to Reid and his school. Reid is, without a doubt, however, of greatest interest to philosophers and historians of philosophy.

As one might suppose from its very name, the philosophy of common sense is doctrinally unexciting. Its basic doctrines are simply the three rudimentary philosophical beliefs of all ordinary men who possess at least the most common degree of understanding: (1) reality is fundamentally an objective world of material objects in space and time; (2) reality is knowable

2. *The Instructed Vision: Scottish common sense Philosophy and the Origins of American Fiction* (Bloomington: Indiana University Press, 1961).

by the human mind; (3) such knowledge is the only sound guide to human action individually and collectively. Of course these beliefs are never, or practically never, given utterance by ordinary men; normally only a philosopher would ever think it worthwhile to formulate them and to investigate their interconnections, implications, and ramifications in order to produce something worthy of being called a philosophy. Nevertheless, they are the common doctrines of common men, in that when articulated they are assented to at once by men of common sense—by men, that is, of normal understanding whose minds have not been tinctured indelibly by superstition, prejudice, or philosophy.

Reid thought that it is particularly the pernicious influence of philosophy that makes it necessary to elaborate and defend a philosophy of common sense; superstition and prejudice are not normally cloaked in respectability, and even when they are they can be exposed relatively easily, although more than exposure is required for their extirpation. But philosophy is a more dangerous foe; it is of noble lineage even when sophistical, its paradoxes are often as delightful as they are subtle, and just by putting the common opinions of the vulgar out of countenance it can pander to the too often overweening self-esteem of the learned.

By "philosophy" Reid understood, primarily, "the received principles" of philosophers from Descartes through Hume. The chief of these principles is the doctrine that Reid calls the "theory of ideas," the claim that we can know nothing about the external world save by means of the "ideas," sensations, impressions, perceptions, or what not that are immediately present to the mind in a way in which external objects cannot be, and which represent the world to us. In one form or another, this principle, Reid thought, has been prevalent, if not universal, among philosophers since Descartes; its fruition is found in Hume's *Treatise of Human Nature*.

Hume was Reid's *bête noir*, and Reid in all his philosophizing has Hume at his most skeptical at the back of his mind. In Berkeley, the skeptical upshot of the "theory of ideas" is the dissolution of the independent spatiotemporal world of material objects into the mind and its contents. According to the canonical interpretation of his philosophy, Hume first accepted Berkeley's results and then tried to resolve the mind into its contents, although admittedly without success. "Ideas seem to have something in their nature unfriendly to other existences," Reid remarked. This tendency toward subjectivism also gets expressed in moral philosophy in the denial of an objective distinction between right and wrong. Moral judgments degenerate into autobiographical remarks about one's own feelings of approbation or disapprobation or, even more primitively, into mere expressions of feeling—moral grunts of approval or groans of dismay.

Many twentieth-century analytic philosophers, especially the more conservative ones, share the Cartesian fulcrum of philosophical argument provided by "the theory of ideas"; at least they share with Descartes and others the fulcrum provided by the theory of ideas as they interpret it. They regard the proper commencement of philosophical analysis to be via "methodological solipsism." Thus, the "problem of the external world" is construed as the problem of how objectivity concepts—material thinghood, unperceived existence, space, etc.—are applied to experience. Ultimately, it is held, this comes down to the problem of how *I* can so organize or interpret *my* experiences that they become my experience of an independent, objective, "external world." This way of beginning philosophical analysis is held to be only methodologically solipsistic because it is merely a mode of analysis and, as such, is independent of particular philosophical theories such as idealism, materialism, mind/body dualism, skepticism, epistemological realism, or whatever. Theories such as these provide various answers to the solipsistic question. By reading this approach back into the history of philosophy, contemporary philosophers are able to claim such philosophers as Berkeley and Hume as progenitors. Thus, Berkeley's denial of the existence of a material world independent of the mind is construed as a needlessly paradoxical way of stating a phenomenalist or quasi-phenomenalist analysis of the "problem of the external world"; similarly, Hume's attempt to dissolve the mind into its contents is construed as partially a denial of an untenable substantival concept of the self and partially as an unsuccessful attempt to provide a correct analysis of the concept of mind.

Reid certainly would have none of this, and probably neither would Berkeley and Hume. Berkeley's notebooks, and his finished writings, are full of uneasy and unconvincing claims that his philosophy is compatible with common sense, and Hume always acknowledged that his philosophy puts philosophy and common sense at odds. Indeed, it is a central feature of Hume's philosophy that the claims of reason and nature (common sense) are irreconcilable. Hume, as much as Reid did or the rest of us do now, believed in the existence of an objective world independent of, and external to, the mind. He said that in such belief he was submitting to the dictates of human nature, but he was not, he thought, consenting to an obvious truth, since reason is capable of concocting insurmountable arguments against accepting this belief as even probably true.

It has sometimes been thought, for example by Kant, that Reid's opposition to the skeptical outcome of previous philosophy has the form of a demagogic crying up of the opinions of the mob, an appeal to an illicit argument from common consent. But Kant apparently knew of Reid only secondhand through the reports of Reid's philosophical enemy, Joseph

Priestly; no impartial reader of Reid's writings can accept Kant's judgment.[3] Reid does stress that in "a matter of common sense, every man is no less a competent judge than a mathematician is in a mathematical demonstration", so that in matters of common sense, philosophers are no better placed than anyone else to judge of the truth of common sense beliefs or, as Reid calls them, "first principles of common sense." But Reid is clear that whether or not a putative first principle really is a belief of common sense, and not merely a widely held prejudice, is not itself a matter of common sense but requires philosophical investigation and argument; one very fertile source of disputes about the first principles of common sense even among men equally well endowed with common sense is that first principles themselves cannot be given apodictical or demonstrative proofs, nor can the claim that a supposed first principle really is a first principle be proved. Reid was always prepared to argue with those who, in any sense, "deny first principles."[4] Even though the philosophical restoration of common sense was his aim, and the appeal to common sense his chief method, Reid was never content to appeal merely to common sense. He was no philosophical philistine.

Although Reid never systematically set out his criteria or "marks" distinguishing the first principle of common sense from common prejudices or other counterfeits, he does mention a number of criteria. Reid is by no means clear on the number of criteria or "marks" or on their logical force, i.e. whether they are severally necessary and jointly sufficient, or whether at best they are merely severally necessary. In any case, the following are the criteria that Reid mentions or uses or both:

1. *The criterion of self-evidence.*[5] Reid does not explain what he means by "self-evident," i.e. self-evident truth, but he certainly does not mean that the self-evident truth of first principles is that of the simple self-evidence of obvious analyticities. Reidian self-evidence seems to decompose analytically into several "marks" of first principles, which he often mentions separately, viz. *(a)* first principles are "no sooner understood than they are believed," at least by men of "ripe understanding"; *(b)* first principles are "the result of our original powers," i.e. our constitution; *(c)* a

3. A German translation of Reid's *Inquiry into the Human Mind* appeared in 1782, a year prior to Kant's attack on Reid in the *Prolegormena to Any Future Metaphysics*. It is not known whether Kant ever read Reid, but his attack is on Reid's views on Hume's analysis of causality, a matter that Reid does not discuss in the *Inquiry*, and that he discussed in print for the first time in 1785 in the *Essays on the Intellectual Powers of Man*. Kant's criticisms of Reid are clearly derived from those of Joseph Priestly in his *Examination of Dr. Reid's "Inquiry"* (1774).

4. The chief locus of Reid's views on the first principles of common sense is in the *Essays on the Intellectual Powers of Man*, Essay 6, "Of Judgment," H 413–75.

5. H 434a–b; H 259b; H 422b; H 425b.

first principle carries "the light of truth in itself," i.e. it stands in no need of external evidence for us to come to believe it. (The metaphor of internal light comes from Plato: the sun illuminates itself as well as everything else; first principles are "self-illuminating.")

2. *The criterion of universal acceptance*.[6] Universal agreement among the unlearned as well as the learned is at least a prima facie sign of the truth of a belief, especially if it is "consent in things not deep nor intricate, but which lie . . . on the surface," unless we can show "some prejudice as universal as that consent is, which might be the cause of it." Reid cites as examples of such universal beliefs our belief in the existence in a material world, the maxim that every change that happens in nature must have a cause, and that there is a right and wrong in human conduct. Such principles are "too universal to be the effects of reasoning," education, or other causes of belief of less than universal scope or operation. Such beliefs are accepted among mankind universally when they are understood clearly and when local and temporary prejudices are removed.

3. *The criterion of irresistibility*.[7] First principles are such that "by the constitution of our nature, we are under a necessity of assenting to them." Reid cites as examples our beliefs in a material world, in other minds, in our freedom to choose, and in the general veracity of our senses. According to Reid, we "cannot live and act according to the rules of common prudence without them." They are as indispensable as they are irresistible. A professional skeptic may doubt that sense perception is reliable, but when his safety is at stake he joins the rest of us in acting as if he knows with absolute certainty that our senses are generally reliable.

4. *The criterion of unprovability*.[8] Because first principles are self-evident they require no proof; because they are fundamental, they do not admit of apodictic or direct demonstrative proof. There are no propositions more fundamental from which they can be derived. Skeptics from Pyrrho and Sextus Empiricus through Hume have shown that first principles such as that sense-perception, memory, and induction are reliable cannot be demonstrated, and that the attempt to do so will produce only inconclusive or fallacious arguments, that usually beg the question.

5. *The criterion of confirmability*.[9] Although the first principles of common sense cannot be proved, they can be confirmed. But because their evidence is intuitive and not demonstrative, "they require to be handled in a way peculiar to themselves"; "they require not proof, but to be placed

6. H 75b; H 233a; H 259a; H 322b; H 438a; H 439b; H 458a.
7. H 108b; H 130a; H 183b; H 230a; H 185a; H 616b.
8. H 230a; H 231a; H 439a–b.
9. H 439a–b; H 231a; H 485a.

in a proper point of view." Just how a first principle can be confirmed depends on the sort of first principle it is. Some first principles are confirmed by showing that their denials are rebarbative to reason by virtue of their manifest absurdity; the skeptical effort to prove by reasoning that there is no force in reason is an example. Moreover, since first principles are interconnected, the part-time skeptic who rejects a particular first principle can be convicted of inconsistency if it can be shown that the first principle he rejects is on a par with others he admits. Such *ad hominem* moves are helpless against total skepticism, but they are effective against the milder forms of skepticism. Thus, "the faculties of consciousness, of memory, of external sense, and of reason are all equally the gifts of nature. No good reason can be assigned for receiving the testimony of one of them, which is not of equal force with regard to the others." So when, in the *Cogito*, Descartes accepts the testimony of consciousness but nevertheless goes on to reject the immediate testimony of sense, he is guilty of an inconsistency, according to Reid. Again, if a philosopher contradicts common sense by breaching the universal forms and usages of language, his doctrine can be rejected as either false, misleading, or unintelligible: if a philosopher says that "color is not a quality of bodies but only an idea in the mind," his claim is false if his words mean what they ordinarily mean, and if they do not, his claim is an unintelligible abuse of language until he explains himself; and even when he does explain his meaning, his claim will be misleading and unnecessarily paradoxical even if it does not actually contradict the first principle that objects really are as we distinctly perceive them to be. Finally, showing that a first principle is so "necessary to the conduct of life" that we cannot live and act according to the rules of common prudence without it confirms the first principle, since it is obviously rational to believe and act on a belief to which there is no alternative.

These five criteria obviously raise problems concerning completeness and adequacy that need investigating, but which are beyond the scope of this introduction to the Orations. But criteria 4 and 5 do require brief comment. Together they help bring out what is perhaps the most distinctive feature of Reid's use of the appeal to common sense, viz., its essential negativity.

Other commonsense philosophers, several of them contemporaneous with Hume and Reid, made the mistake of rising to the skeptics' bait by trying to construct strict proofs of such commonsense first principles as that those things really did happen which we distinctly remember to have happened; that those things do really exist which we distinctly perceive by our senses and are what we perceive them to be; that the natural faculties by which we distinguish truth from error are not fallacious; or that there is life and intelligence in our fellow men with whom we converse. Reid considered any such positive enterprise to be fundamentally misconceived. Such first principles are only contingent, and contingent propositions can be inferred only from other contingent propositions; the problem of establishing their truth would only be pushed back a step even if we could derive such first principles from other contingent propositions. But if these are genuine first principles, they cannot be given demonstrative proofs—this, partly, is what is meant by calling them first principles: they are at rock bottom. Although these and most other first principles are only contingent and hence conceivably false, Reid thinks they are true, and even self-evidently true. Any attempt to derive them from other contingencies that are not self-evidently true would necessarily fail since such "proofs" would have to rely on propositions less obvious and less known than the principle to be demonstrated. It is no wonder that skeptics are so successful in their arguments; they raise the impossible demand that the beliefs of common sense be proved and then, correctly in Reid's view, counter every deluded attempt to satisfy this demand with devastating objections.

Reid's consistent refusal to be drawn into the skeptic's trap while at the same time avoiding the outrageous dogmatism of his disciples James Beattie and James Oswald is a model of philosophical moderation. Reid, always methodologically self-conscious, in his well-known letter to Hume, where he avows himself a disciple of Hume in metaphysics, wrote, "In attempting to throw some new light upon those abstruse subjects, I wish to preserve the due mean betwixt confidence and despair," i.e. between dogmatism and total nihilistic skepticism. Criterion 4 innoculates us against dogmatism, while criterion 5 preserves us from total skepticism. It is an interesting question that needs investigating as to whether this feature of Reid's philosophy brings him closer to the much-softened "mitigated scepticism" of Hume's later *Enquiry Concerning Human Understanding* than either Reid or Hume realized.[10]

Reid also has a "Newtonian" or scientific defense of common sense directed against Hume at his skeptical best, or worst, as Reid saw it. Roughly, the story is this: Hume, accepting skeptical arguments that we cannot justify our natural belief in the existence of the external world (etc., *mutatis mutandis* for our other natural beliefs) either by showing it to be a dictate of reason or by deducing it from the data of the senses, sets aside the question of justification and proposes instead to answer the more tractable question *"What causes induce us to believe in the existence of body?"*[11]

10. Louise Marcil-Lacoste has begun this investigation in "The Seriousness of Reid's Sceptical Admissions" in *Monist* 61 no. 2 (April 1978): 311–21.

11. Hume, *Treatise of Human Nature*, ed. L. A. Selby-Bigge (Oxford, Clarendon Press 1888), bk. 1, pt. 4, sec. 2, pp. 187–218.

Hume takes it for granted that causal explanations of our natural beliefs do not justify them just because he accepts various skeptical arguments that all such beliefs are unjustifiable. Reid can be understood as challenging Hume on his own ground, i.e. as attempting to answer Hume's causal questions in causal terms that both explain and justify our natural beliefs.

The gist of Reid's position is something like this: A causal account of why we have a belief can justify that belief if the cause that produces it is of the right kind. Commonsense beliefs have justifying causes, but transient opinion, superstition, and skeptical philosophical opinions do not. An inductive study of the opinions and behavior of men at the level of ordinary everyday practice enables us to sort out and distinguish those beliefs belonging to common sense from other common but disreputable sorts of belief with which commonsense beliefs are often confused. Ordinary commonsense beliefs, when analyzed, can be shown to follow from certain "first principles," some of which are contingent, others necessary. These first principles are intuitive judgments such that we are caused to believe them immediately upon understanding them, provided that the mind is not disordered by madness, superstition, or an undue fondness for a captious skepticism or other *idola mentis*. To understand them at all is to believe that they are true. The intuitive first principles are understood as self-evident; there is no searching and weighing of evidence and arguments, nor can they be deduced or inferred from other, more basic, propositions. Both the judgments of first principles and our belief in them are the work of nature and result from the operations of such constitutive powers of the mind as memory, conception, sense perception, and reason. Such intuitive judgments and our belief in them are, so to speak, protophenomena of the mind, brute constitutional facts of the epistemic powers with which we are endowed by nature.

Reid believes that the intuitive first principles of common sense satisfy the reality and sufficiency requirements for a sound theory; they are real because they are discovered by inductive-cum-logical analysis, and they are sufficient both for producing and for justifying our untutored commonsense beliefs. Their inherent self-evidence is sufficient to cause our beliefs; no other causes need be brought in to explain why we believe them. But it is not simply that we *do* believe the natural and intuitive judgments of common sense, or even that we *must* believe them (Hume allows this much); we are also fully justified in believing them because, Reid believes, at the level of protophenomena of the mind, in the domain of the cognitive/ intellectual powers, no legitimate distinction can be made between brute facts and brute prescriptions. We do, we must, and we ought to believe in and act upon the first principles of common sense, at least until God endows us with new and better faculties that can sit in judgment on the deliverances of the old. The first principles of common sense are, on Reid's analysis, both descriptive and prescriptive or normative laws of the constitution of man's intellect determining and constraining the conditions of belief formation and belief acquisition.

In some ways, Reid's assertion of first principles of common sense as self-evident truths is comparable to Wittgenstein's "this language-game is played" or "what has to be accepted, the given, is—so one could say—*forms of life*." Like Wittgenstein, Reid looks upon our ordinary, everyday, commonsense language, behavior, and beliefs as "protophenomena." Skeptical attacks on the first principles that underlie everyday common sense are not to be answered by trying to provide them with philosophical underpinnings in the form of "proofs." Instead, Reid, again like Wittgenstein, engages in the proper philosophical tasks of criticizing skeptical arguments in detail and analyzing or exhibiting as amply as he can the array of conceptual interconnections among first principles and construing their connections with the activities with which they are interwoven. In this way, Reid tries to show us how costly accepting skepticism would be. For Reid, this is about as far as philosophy-as-justification can go.

Reid was also well aware of the Wittgensteinian point that explanations must come to a halt somewhere. We simply do not know how we manage to perceive the external world, remember past events, or how we are able to exercise various other intellectual powers. We just do. One of his most insistent criticisms of the theory of ideas is that the introduction of "ideas" as mediating entities in the mind's transactions with the external world does not actually explain anything. Question: How do we see objects at a distance from us? Answer: Indirectly via our immediate acquaintance with ideas (or impressions or sensations, etc.) that represent them to us. Question: But how can we ever bridge the ontological gap between the ideas and the material world to be sure that ideas really do perform this function and that they do so adequately? Enter Berkeley, exit the material world. But Berkeley's metaphysical world of minds and their ideas is not good enough, according to Reid, if only because it is not really such a world at all; at a critical point it collapses into solipsism. It was left to Hume to try to dispose of even that lonely solipsistic mind.

In an essay of this length, it is not possible to give an adequate account of even one of the many interesting and important facets of Reid's philosophy. I focus here on the philosophical appeal to common sense because Reid does not discuss this key element in his philosophy at any significant length in the Orations and partly because I disucss other matters below in my commentary on the Orations. But his use of the appeal to common sense is by no means the whole of Reid's philosophy. Reid thought of himself as an underlaborer clearing away an accumulation of rubbish impeding the progress of philosophy and, thus, was led to deny having any positive philosophical theories of his own to offer in place of those he criticizes and rejects. He was not being disingenuous. Nevertheless, the makings of distinctively commonsense philosophical theories are to be found in abundance in his writings, and two of these bodies of workable ore ought to be mentioned: First, Reid's discussions of sensation and perception in the *Inquiry into the Human Mind* and the *Essays on the Intellectual Powers* are rich in material for constructing a supple and subtle perceptual realism. Second, his criticism of Hume's moral philosophy, in the *Active Powers*, is as well argued, and as sound as any that have been given since, and provides an adequate *terminus a quo* from which a commonsense philosophy of morals can be developed. Philosophers and laymen alike will find a lot of substance in Reid's works in every area of philosophy except formal logic.

I

Reid's Philosophical Orations (1753, 1756, 1759, 1762) were delivered in Latin at Graduation ceremonies in King's College as part of his duties under the so-called regenting system. Under this system of instruction, a regent took charge of a group of students after a first year of instruction in Greek and, as their sole teacher, conducted them through the next three years of their university education. Thus, a regent would teach a class of students all their subjects. Reid taught natural science and mathematics as well as logic, metaphysics, political philosophy, and ethics while regenting in Aberdeen. At the end of their fourth year, students would be promoted for graduation by their teacher. At each graduation exercise, Reid delivered an Oration summing up his general philosophical position and doctrines.

The original manuscript of the Philosophical Orations is in the Birkwood manuscript collection in the Library of King's College, University of Aberdeen (MS K222). Reid obviously did not intend the Orations for publication. They exhibit the marks of occasional rhetoric and looseness of organization, a tendency to floridity, and they contain far too many learned allusions, many of them somewhat obscure. According to Shirley Darcus Sullivan, translator for this edition, and W. R. Humphries, editor of the 1937 Latin edition published by the University of Aberdeen Press, Reid's manuscripts are sufficiently full of errors in Latin, and of purely rhetorical punctuation devices, to indicate that Reid did not contemplate publishing his Orations. As an academic Scot, Reid would have been much too proud of the renown of Scottish Latinity to have allowed the manuscript to be published in its present state.

The present English-language edition was translated and prepared for publication on the basis of the Humphries 1937 Latin text. Humphries' text was checked against a clear photocopy of the original manuscript provided by Colin A. McLaren, archivist and keeper of manuscripts for the University of Aberdeen, and was found to be a careful and accurate transcription of the manuscripts.

The Philosophical Orations are of interest and importance to historians as well as philosophers. Traditionally, Reid is held to have combined a fierce loyalty to the traditional regenting system of instruction[12] with an equally intense zeal for curriculum reform. The Orations, particularly Oration II, provide some evidence of both these attitudes. His extravagant eulogies of Bacon and Newton and his generous praise of Locke and Hume, even though he considered them usually to be more wrong than right, together with his severe strictures against medieval Aristotelianism show that Reid was a thoroughly modern thinker. On the other hand, when Reid deplores the development of professional specialization and argues for the fellowship of philosophy and the common arts, even to the extent of elevating this supposed fellowship to the status of a "law" of the nature of philosophy (see especially Oration II),[13] we probably are being presented with an oblique defense of the traditional system of instruction. In any event, the Orations provide us with important evidence of the nature of instruction in an important Scottish school in the mid-eighteenth century. We know from other evidence—the minutes of the college senate—that two years after Reid began teaching in King's College, significant curricular reforms were initiated. Traditional syllogistics and metaphysics were downgraded, and the arts faculty were enjoined to spend more time on "those parts of Philosophy which may qualifie men for the more useful and important offices of Society." Reid is reported as concurring in this reform; it seems likely that he did so with some enthusiasm.[14]

The Philosophical Orations are also of historical and philosophical interest in other ways. They throw considerable light on the early phases of Reid's philosophy and serve to show how Reid's later works were not so much developments of his early views as amplifications and elaborations

---

12. The regenting system was abolished in King's College in 1784.

13. See Oration II, pp. 46–47 below.

14. For extremely interesting and valuable discussions of the status and role of philosophy in the Scottish University systems, and particularly of the Philosophy of common sense, see G. E. Davie, *The Democratic Intellect*, (Edinburgh: Edinburgh University Press), 1961.

of them. As Humphries notes, "These four Orations are as characteristic of Reid as anything of his that we possess."[15] It is, I believe, clear from a scrutiny of these Orations that the 'late' Reid is distinguished from the 'early' Reid not by a chronology of reversed or seriously revised opinions but by a deepened and strengthened maturity in philosophical sophistication. The Third Oration is particularly fine as a concise statement of Reid's main criticisms of the "theory of ideas" in, mainly, Locke, Berkeley, and Hume. The Orations are also valuable to historians of philosophy as an introduction to the philosophy of science of the man who was "pre-eminently the philosopher of science in the eighteenth century."[16]

The Philosophical Orations fall naturally into two groups. The first and second Orations are chiefly concerned with the philosophy of science and philosophical methodology. The third and fourth Orations are focused on criticism of the "theory of ideas" and on various related topics in the philosophy of mind. With the exception of Oration III, the Orations are too brief to be summarized usefully; indeed, they are summaries. Instead, I shall comment briefly on various matters raised in or by the Orations.

Orations I and II

Oration I is very sketchy and quite extraordinarily crude. This might be because Reid took charge of the pupils of Alexander Rait during their third year of instruction and so, perhaps, had less to say than he might have, had he been fully in charge of his pupils for the usual period. In any case some of the notable features of Oration I are:

1. Reid has a general tendency to equivocate on what by the eighteenth century had become, or nearly so, separate meanings of "philosophy." Reid does not often distinguish clearly between philosophy proper and "natural philosophy" or science. The reader is cautioned to supply the distinction where appropriate.

2. Reid's descanting on Bacon and, especially, Newton is a noteworthy, if sometimes exasperating, feature not only of these Orations but of practically all of Reid's works. Dugald Stewart in his *Life of Thomas Reid* (1803) says, rightly, I think, that one of the important distinguishing fea-

15. W. R. Humphries, ed., *Philosophical Orations of Thomas Reid* (Aberdeen: Aberdeen University Press, 1937), p. 7. This view has been disputed, but not unproblematically, by John Immerwahr in "The Development of Reid's Realism" in *Monist* 61, no. 2, (April 1978). Immerwahr sets out clearly some of the issues in the "static" versus "developmental" views of Reid's works, especially as regards Reid's theory of perception.

16. R. W. Harris, *Reason and Nature in Eighteenth-Century Thought*, (London: Blandford Press, 1968), p. 411.

tures of Reid's philosophy is the systematic steadiness of his adherence to what he thought of as Baconian-cum-Newtonian principles. It is this rather than any personal contributions to the stock of philosophical ideas that makes Reid preeminently the philosopher of science of his time.[17]

Reid, of course, was not alone in his extravagant regard for Newtonian physics and in his desire to see all the sciences brought to a state of what he thought of as Newtonian perfection. The philosophical and popular literature of the time was almost idolatrous in the respect and admiration shown for Newton. Nor was Reid alone in his mistaken belief that Newton's inductivism was continuous with Baconian inductivism and, indeed, the culmination and perfection of a scientific method first discovered by Bacon. The fact is that Baconian and Newtonian inductivism have little but the word in common. Both relied on observation and "induced" their results from those observations, but there the similarity ends. Bacon's rules of induction were for the purpose of "discovering" real definitions of the essences of things *per genus et differentia*. Newton's *Regulae Philosophandi* were methods for discovering, and formulating in a form useful for physics, the universal causal laws governing the workings of nature. Bacon really ought to be viewed as the last of the great medieval scientists, not the first of the moderns. In any case, Reid's error is not a serious one, since it was Newton's inductivist principles and not Bacon's that Reid did so much to promote.

3. Reid's attacks on "hypotheses" in "philosophy" are very frequently attacks on fanciful theorizing as a substitute for induction and observation in the sciences rather than attacks on hypotheses as such. In the *Intellectual Powers*, Reid assigns to hypotheses the role of suggesting experiments and directing our inquiries, but holds that "just induction" alone should govern our beliefs.[18] Sometimes, however, Reid means something more definite by "hypotheses," viz., theories purporting to explain some phenomenon such that (1) the causes or explanatory entities cannot be shown to exist and (2) would not explain the phenomenon even if they did exist. These two features of "hypotheses" violate the conditions of adequacy of explanation laid down in the first of Newton's *Regulae Philosophandi*: "We are to admit no more causes of natural things than such as are both true and sufficient to explain their appearance."[19] Reid regards Newton's *Regulae* as maxims of common sense. His attacks on "mere hypotheses" are designed

17. For an excellent discussion of Reid as a philosopher of science, see L. L. Laudon's "Thomas Reid and the Newtonian Turn of British Methodological Thought," in Butts and Davis, eds., *The Methodological Heritage of Newton* (Toronto: University of Toronto Press, 1970).

18. H 251a.

19. *Mathematical Principles of Natural Philosophy* (Berkeley: University of California Press, 1947), p. 398.

to assist him in criticism of the "theory of ideas," which he attempts to characterize as a "hypothesis" and, thus, as contrary to common sense and Newtonian principles of scientific method. The obvious objection to Reid's procedure is that the philosophical theory of ideas is not a causal or scientific theory, but Reid is aware of this and intends his views on hypotheses to apply to all kinds of explanation. He argues subsequently, in Orations III and IV,[20] that ideas do not exist and would not explain the operation of the human mind even if they did.

4. Reid's strictures against "dialectic or scholastic logic" in the last third of the first Oration clearly are misplaced. He treats logic almost as if it is a material science and criticizes it for failure to be fruitful of objective discoveries. He demonstrates here the same mistaken criticism of the theory of syllogistic that he makes at length in his *A Brief Account of Aristotle's Logic* (chap. 4, sec. 5) "On this theory considered as an Engine of Science."[21] Perhaps the severity of our judgment of Reid's views can be mitigated if we keep in mind that he had constantly in view, as enemies to be kept at bay, the schoolmen whose philosophy, even in the eighteenth century, was an impediment to the development of science. Reid must be faulted but not too harshly. He certainly ought to have known that the scholastic logicians did not regard the syllogistic as an instrument for making empirical discoveries, and had he known it he could have avoided the absurdity of censuring formal logic for failing to deliver what no competent logician ever claimed for it. Even so, Reid's keen appreciation of mathematics and of the role of mathematics in natural science, together with his awareness that most mathematical reasoning could not be forced into forms that would be acknowledged by the logicians of the day, excuses most of Reid's erroneous assessment by formal logic. After all, he cannot be condemned for his ignorance of developments in logic that were to occur only a century or so later. In any case, Reid was in good company in his errors; similar views of scholastic logic were held by Descartes, Bacon, the Port Royal logicians, and Locke.

Oration II is somewhat more philosophically interesting, if not much more substantial, than Oration I. Reid had announced his intention in the first Oration to offer some observations on the "laws of practicing philosophy," but in fact got only so far as to tell us that such laws are to be sought from the nature and purpose of the activity as exemplified in the best work of the best philosophers of the past. In Oration II, he proposes to discuss "some very general laws of philosophy by which we can separate philosophy that is true, genuine, and worthy of its name from empty,

20. See pp. 60–64; 73 ff. below.
21. H 701–2.

counterfeit and illegitimate philosophy."[22] He declines to discuss any "laws" of philosophizing that are proper to particular branches of philosophy. The following is, I believe, fair commentary:

1. The first and second of Reid's "laws of practicing philosophy" merit little comment. When Reid tells us that (1) "all futile questions and disputes must be removed from philosophy," either he is being quite trivial or he is begging important questions. And when he says that (2) "the philosopher will think that no knowledge, wisdom, or art that is useful to the human race is alien to himself," which he says is "a law closely akin to the first,"[23] he is again either begging questions or, depending on how this vague "law" is interpreted, uttering a paltry truth or a blatant falsehood. In any case, it is impossible to muster any sympathy for Reid's elevation of these observations, even construed at their best, to the grand status of "laws of practicing philosophy." Reid's remarks, however, do indicate something of the strong pragmatist tendency in his philosophy.[24] In the *Active Powers*, Reid insists that knowledge derives its value from enlarging our powers of action. It is "the very intention of our being" to manage our active powers by proposing to ourselves the best ends, planning the most proper system of conduct in our power, and executing it industriously and zealously. "This is true wisdom," according to Reid.[25]

2. Reid's third "law of practicing philosophy," viz. (3), "the philosopher is forbidden to play the role of the poet or to invade the sacred privileges of the bards,"[26] does not merit being called a law, but at least it verges on the heuristic. It sums up Reid's frequently expressed abhorrence of the resort by philosophers to fanciful conjectures and hypotheses (in Reid's pejorative sense) when faced with difficulties. Officially, Reid regards all such imaginative conjectures as counterfeits of evidence or as ersatz ratiocination.[27] In practice, however, Reid, like other philosophers, is sometimes prepared to resort to imaginative thought-experiments to clarify a concept or make a point. A notable example is found in the *Inquiry* (chap. 6, sec. 9) "of the Geometry of Visibles," where Reid imagines "the Idomenians," an order of very intelligent beings possessing only one sense modality,

22. See pp. 41 below.
23. See pp. 45 below.
24. C. S. Peirce, the father of pragmatism, or as he called it, pragmaticism, calls Reid "that subtle but well balanced intellect", and unhesitatingly claims Reid's philosophy of common sense as the immediate ancestor of his own views. See "Critical Common-Sensism" in *Collected Papers of Charles Sanders Peirce*, ed. Charles Hartsharne and Paul Weiss (Cambridge, Mass.: Harvard University Press, 1960) 5:293–305.
25. H 511.
26. See p. 47 below.
27. Hamilton notes that Reid and Kant hold the same doctrine of the incompatibility of the creative imagination and philosophy. See H 99b, fn.

viz., that of sight. In a sustained train of imagination, Reid there develops a geometry of visibles appropriate to such a tribe as part of his reply to Berkeley's denial that a geometry of visibles is possible.[28] I am loath, however, to charge Reid with inconsistency. His most strongly expressed warnings against "the creative imagination" in philosophy are directed against the practice of positing explanatory entities and then going on to theorize about some matter without in the end having determined that the postulated entities actually do exist and actually do function as described in the theory. Only memory, sense perception, and consciousness are "original principles" or sources of legitimate existential beliefs, according to Reid. Imagination is at best a form of "simple apprehension" of its objects, lacking all existential implications and, hence, is no proper source of belief.[29] His targets in his attacks on the use of the imagination in philosophy are usually the Scholastics, and Locke, Berkeley, and Hume as advocates of a "theory of ideas." Reid thought that there is no good reason at all for thinking that "ideas" of the kind required actually exist. (See discussion of Reid on "the theory of ideas" in my commentary on Oration III, below.) But the use of the imagination by Reid and other philosophers in constructing thought-experiments or in devising counterexamples is a different matter and need not be regarded as running afoul of Reid's "third law."

3. Reid's fourth and fifth laws of practicing philosophy are (4) "the philosopher does not busy himself in overthrowing common notions," and (5) philosophy is "not only to refrain from opposing common notions, but also [is] to be erected and built upon them."[30]

Reid does not provide any examples of "common notions" in this Oration, but in the *Intellectual Powers* (chiefly essay 6, "Of Judgment," pp. 413–75), where "common notions" are promoted to the post of first principles, he lists twelve first principles of contingent truths and six types of first principles of necessary truths, with a number of examples. Some examples of the first principles of contingent truths are "the existence of everything of which I am conscious," "those things did really happen which I distinctly remember," and "the natural faculties by which we distinguish truth from error, are not fallacious." Examples of two types of first principles of necessary truth are, in morals, "a generous action has more merit than a merely just one" and, in metaphysics, "whatever begins to exist must have a cause which produced it."

Reid's fourth and fifth laws are hardly descriptive laws encapsulating the actual practice of most philosophers or precepts that a great many philos-

---

28. H 147b–52a.
29. H 106b.
30. See pp. 49–51 below.

ophers would accept as binding. They are, however, quintessentially Reidian doctrines and methodological precepts. They raise problems of a magnitude that Reid could not have been expected to deal with in the Orations.[31] For example: How are common notions or first principles related to common sense? Is common sense an intellectual faculty or a nonrational natural instinct as Hume claimed, or, in a somewhat Kantian fashion, something the possession of which is necessary to the existence of mind as such? Are the common notions or first principles of contingent truths in some way synthetic a priori, or are they perhaps very high-powered empirical generalizations? What precisely are the functions of first principles? Reid had a strong mathematical bent, and he often treats first principles as extraordinarily fertile axioms of all human thought, exercising their governance in ways analogous to the way the nature of the axioms of a deductive system limits the kind of theorems permissible in a system. Occasionally, however, he seems to have thought of first principles as tacit presuppositions silently infusing human thought with metaphysical coherence—metaphysical threads of Ariadne or, perhaps, metaphysical vincula. In either case, first principles would be fundamental regulators of thought. But in which, if either of these lights ought we to view them? In the Orations, Reid equivocates, and no answer is vouchsafed. During the period in which Reid was delivering these triennial Orations, he was writing his first major published work, *An Inquiry into the Human Mind, on the Principles of Common Sense* (1764). Reid frequently appeals to common sense in the *Inquiry* in support of his views on sense perception or in criticism of other philosophers, but he nowhere in this book subjects the concept of common sense itself to analysis. Apparently, Reid came to see this as a deficiency in the *Inquiry*, for by 1768 or 1769, he was working on the topic of common sense, and he read a paper that he called a *"Curâ Prima on Common Sense"* to the Literary Society of Glasgow.[32] In this *"Curâ Prima,"* Reid defends the view that common sense is a faculty of the understanding, an intellectual power, and in the *Intellectual Powers* (1785) he says that common sense is an office or degree of reason, viz., the power

31. For an interesting and detailed, although not, I think, entirely satisfactory account of Reid's theories of common sense and first principles, see S. A. Grave's *The Scottish Philosophy of Common Sense*, (Oxford: Oxford University Press, 1960), esp. chaps. 3, 4. Louise Marcil Lacoste's discussion of Reid's theory of common sense in her excellent book *Claude Buffier and Thomas Reid: Two Common-Sense Philosophy* (Kingston and Montreal: McGill-Queen's University Press, 1982), demonstrates the close connection of Reid's theory of common sense with his inductive Newtonionism in a way that significantly clarifies both those aspects of Reid's philosophy.

32. For the text of Reid's *"Curâ Prima,"* ed. David F. Norton and a preface by Norton with a very useful discussion, see the Appendix to Marcil-Lacoste's *Claude Buffier and Thomas Reid*, pp. 179–208.

to judge of things self-evident.[33] His implicit target is Hume who regards common sense as a nonrational natural instinct producing its beliefs more or less mechanically, certainly without thought or regard for truth. In the *Intellectual Powers*, Reid shifts his attention to the epistemic functions of the first principles discerned by common sense, but he does not revise or abandon his views of common sense as a rational power of the mind.

Reid remains consistent in his views of the role of common sense in philosophy from the inchoate formulations of these fourth and fifth laws of practicing philosophy through the stage of the "*Curâ Prima*" to the maturity of the *Intellectual Powers*. Common sense as a practical faculty oriented toward the banal affairs of everyday life has no serious critics among philosophers. As a theoretical faculty with pretensions to exercising constraints on our liberty to philosophize, common sense has always been alluring to some philosophers and repugnant to others. Both parties will find a lot to think about in Reid's views on the matter.

Orations III and IV

1. The dominant theories of knowledge of the day held in common, in one or another version, the doctrine that the immediate objects of the mind's awareness, in all its operations (perception, memory, judgment etc.), are "ideas". Reid thinks that the doctrine is false and that its adoption leads to philosophically calamitous consequences. At the worst, it results, he thinks, in total Humean skepticism and, at best, in Berkelian immaterialism. Reid views Locke's theories as rickety compromises between the demands of this "theory of ideas" and the pull of Locke's healthy common sense. Orations III and IV contain Reid's most concise statement of his objections to the "theory of ideas." These objections are raised mainly in connection with an examination of the nature of judgment and apprehension. It seems rather odd, but theories of sensation and perception in which "ideas" (sensations, impressions, etc.) played a conceptually central role from Descartes through Hume get short shrift in these Orations, despite the fact that during the same period in which the Orations were delivered, Reid was reading to the Aberdeen Philosophical Society the papers that later became the *Inquiry into the Human Mind* that was devoted almost entirely to the theory of perception.

The entire drift of philosophy from Descartes onward with the ultimate sundering of reason and nature and a forlorn skepticism as its main results,

---

33. H 425b. See also H 434a.

is a consequence of the adoption of the "theory of ideas" as our explanatory device, Reid thinks. But from the beginning, the theory of ideas was in conflict with common sense because it entails that we are never directly in cognitive contact with reality. Berkeley's attempted salvage of the theory failed, and it required only the relentless logic of Hume to make the break between common sense and philosophy complete and, so Hume thought, irreparable.

The main features of Reid's attack on the common doctrine of ideas can be stated briefly and straightforwardly.[34] His strategy is to show that the ideal theory is a hypothesis (in Reid's pejorative sense of the term explained above). Reid, with considerable historical justification, consistently understands "ideas" in the philosophical theory of ideas to be "images in the mind," or, in one version, "in the brain." His argument is that introspection does not reveal the contents of the mind—judgments, memories, sensations,—to be images, and observation of perceptible objects, including images in the literal sense of the term, e.g. representational pictures or sculpture, reveals nothing distinctively mental about them. Since neither of these two sources of our knowledge of the mind and of the world acquaints us with ideas, there is no positive evidence for their existence. Thus, the "ideal theory" falls afoul of the first part of Newton's requirements for explanatory adequacy. The theory of ideas also fails to satisfy the demands of the second part of Newton's first rule for philosophizing—even if there were ideas, they would not help us to explain the operations of the mind. Ideas are introduced to help explain how the mind's operations can be directed upon things that are distant in space (perception) or remote in time and now nonexistent (memory) or up on things thought about but altogether absent from one's present perception, and on things thought about but which have never existed. The explanation is supposed to be that in these operations the mind is directed upon ideas which function immediately as representatives or signs or, perhaps, symbols of things external to, and remote from, the mind. This is essentially the Lockean theory. But ideas simply cannot serve this function *tout court*; they require interpreting, and there is nothing in the nature of an idea or image (granting their existence for the sake of discussion) or in the theory of ideas that would enable us to know that an interpretation on a particular occasion is correct. Not only does the theory of ideas not help us to explain the powers of the mind, but it also wantonly complicates the very phenomena to be explained. Reid says that it was to Berkeley's credit to see this but thoroughly wrong of him to accept ideas as immediate objects of the mind at the cost of giving up a mind-independent reality.

34. See pp. 58 below.

Reid has a number of interesting and quite possibly correct explanations of how philosophers might originally have been led into the theory of ideas. Analogies between the operations of the mind and the operations of physical bodies are common in ordinary language. "Understand," "conceive," "imagine," "comprehend," "deliberate," "infer," and many other words of this kind were all borrowed originally from our talk about the operations of bodies. It may be, Reid thinks, that when we philosophize we are imposed upon by those analogies and are caught up in trailing clouds of etymology, as J. L. Austin puts it. Since bodies cannot act on each other unless they are in contact with each other directly or indirectly through an intervening series of other bodies or other material media, it would be only natural for someone under the powerful influence of the mind-body analogies built into ordinary language to posit intervening media—ideas—by means of which the mind in sense perception interacts with objects at a distance from us in space or, in memory, at a distance in time. Immediately experienced impressions, sensations, or "ideas" are, supposedly, just such intervening media. Thus, when I remember having eaten eggs for breakfast yesterday, I cannot possibly be in cognitive contact with that now non-existent event, so I must be cognitively in contact with something else which does exist now, at the time of my remembering, and which represents yesterday's breakfast to me, an "idea" of my having eaten eggs for breakfast yesterday. And when I see my desk across the room some feet away, my mind cannot be in direct contact with that slightly distant object; I am *here*, it is over *there*. So, I must be in indirect contact with the desk through the medium of sensations, sense impressions, or visual "ideas" which function to represent the table to my mind.

Reid thinks that just such mind-body analogies motivate "the ideal theory."[35] He was deeply suspicious of the practice, common among ordinary men as well as philosophers, of modeling the language we use to talk about the characteristics of the mind on the language used to talk about bodies.[36] In the first place, such analogies involve a *petitio principii*. They beg the important philosophical question whether mental and physical events are sufficiently similar to justify attributing similar characteristics to them, especially similar modes of operation. Moreover, Reid notes, if the mind-body analogy underlying the ideal theory is accepted as correct, then the ideal theory (in its Lockean form anyway) is no better than a truncated form of the medieval Aristotelian theory of perception, according to which,

35. See pp. 72 ff. below.
36. See especially H 236–38. Those views of Reid are, of course, not original. He learned them from Berkeley and, perhaps, also from Arnauld. Cf. *Principles of Human Knowledge,* sec. 144.

objects are perceived by means of a chain of connected "sensible species" running from the sensible object to the mind of the perceiver. Ideas in the mind bring us no closer to objects than we would be without them, so that still other objects (sensible species) running right up to the body perceived seem to be called for. But this would be to revive the very medieval Aristotelianism to which the theory of ideas is supposed to be the glorious and triumphant modern alternative. Those "little images fluttering through the air," to which Descartes referred with such scorn, are actually indispensable to the ideal theory of mental representation, Reid believes, if it is to avoid Hume's skeptical development of Berkeley's immaterialism.

Reid hoped that his strenuous opposition to the "theory of ideas" would help clear the way for a careful application of scientific procedures to whatever problems in the philosophy of mind turn out to be amenable to them. He believed that a scientific psychology might someday lay bare the "laws of our constitution." Even then, explanations are likely to come to a halt in a way that is unsatisfying to a certain cast of mind. If, for example, the physiology of perception were ever to develop to the extent that we came to know the empirically necessary and sufficient conditions for the occurrence of vision, we would still not know why just *those* conditions, and not others, result in the experience of sight. We should just have to accept that it is so. Moreover, Reid is confident that the development of science cannot subvert our commonsense belief that we perceive the world directly. A developed and adequate physiology of perception would not explain *away* our visual experience of the external world or call into question the truth of the first principle that perception puts us in cognitive contact with an extramental reality, simply because such a scientific theory would ultimately have to rely on the veracity of pretheoretical sense perception to get its start. Whatever the outcome of scientific developments might eventually be, Reid is confident that we will have to continue to rely on sundry first principles of common sense as the foundations of our most general scientific and philosophic outlook. In Reid's view, science is common sense disciplined, extended, and amplified beyond its untutored natural limits. As such, it does not nullify common sense no matter how strange and wondrous its discoveries might turn out to be. He believes that organized scientific activity (theorizing-cum-experimentation) differs only in level of sophistication, i.e. only in degree, from ordinary everyday common sense prudential activity in dealing with the world, and that the propositional yield of the two can differ only in sophistication, so that science cannot yield propositions in conflict with the first principles of common sense.[37]

37. H 484a–b.

Clearly Reid's criticisms of the ideal theory do not prove that it is false; for all that he says in these arguments, some form of the theory might be true despite both the lack of evidence in favor of the theory and its inutility in explanations of mental phenomena. Even so, Reid does give us fairly persuasive considerations against adopting any theory of mental representation that is subject to these criticisms.

2.[38] A few remarks ought to be made about Reid's comments on ideas interpreted as "images in the brain." Reid has been severely criticized by commentators for supposing that any ideal theorist ever meant quite literally that to have an idea is to have a small picture imprinted on the flesh of the brain.[39] In defense of Reid, it should be pointed out that some of the views of David Hartley (1705–57) in *Observations on Man, His Frame, His Duty, and His Expectations* (London, 1749) are subject to a materialistic interpretation and were so interpreted by many in the eighteenth century. The "images-in-the-brain" version of the ideal theory is a conceivable form of a crude materialist theory of mind/body identity. Reid's criticism in the Orations and in the *Intellectual Powers*[40] is effective against any such crude form of identity thesis: (1) taken quite literally, the theory is just plainly false; dissection of brains does not reveal anything in them resembling images of external objects; (2) it is impossible to see what, if any, intelligible meaning can be assigned to "image." On any intelligible meaning, an "image" ought to resemble that of which it is an image, and certainly the impressions on the brain (which everyone admits accompany our experiences) do not resemble anything outside the brain. So, the expression "image in the brain" seems either to have no factual application or to be unintelligible. (3) Moreover, on one possible version of the theory in which ideas are not the having of brain images but perceivings of them, we are asked to believe what is contrary to experience, viz., that we never perceive external objects but only our own brains. Reid's reply to this is very like a reply by G. E. Moore to a similar doctrine once held by Bertrand Russell:[41] I have never perceived my brain at all; this table I now see is not part of my brain. Put linguistically, Reid's reply is that if the language with which the philosophers' claim is made means what it ordinarily means, then the philosopher's claim is simply a misdescription of the facts. But if

---

38. The following is not entirely exegetical; it involves a reconstruction of Reid's views from his *Intellectual Powers of Man* as well as from the Philosophical Orations. See pp. 68–73 below, and H 202a–b.

39. Most recently by S. A. Grave in *The Scottish Philosophy of Common Sense*, p. 18.

40. H 248–53.

41. Cf. Bertrand Russell, *The Analysis of Matter* (London: George Allen & Unwin Ltd., 1927), p. 383.

it does not mean what it ordinarily means, language is being wantonly abused, and we are being given words without meaning.

3. Several other features of Orations III and IV should be noted. Reid's rather curious theologically inspired agnosticism is prominent in the Orations as in his other writings. Throughout his works, Reid officially disclaims any theoretical pretensions and declines to offer Reidian theories of the mind and its cognitive powers, although in fact various philosophical theories or fragments of theories can be extracted from his writings. In any case, he claims that such mental operations as memory, judgment, perception, etc., are "original," "simple and undefinable" and thus are inexplicable by analysis or by reference to anything else such as brain states or whatever. But Reid is no antiscientific obscurantist. He allows that by observation and experiment we will someday arrive at correct descriptions and characterizations of the powers of the mind and at correct accounts of the physiological and other conditions that accompany the functioning of the mind's powers and in the absence of which the mind's powers are inoperative. It is only natural to wonder what Reid can possibly mean by "explanation." Normally, we think that to describe a phenomenon correctly and to set out the conditions under which it occurs, and so on, is just to give the laws of its nature and to explain it, i.e. to make it more familiar or to render its relations to other things more familiar. To do this is to acquire the ability to make predictions about the phenomenon and, in many cases, to exercise some control over it. All of this is just what it is to have explanations and understanding of phenomena. Why then does Reid not allow that we can explain, say, sense perception or memory?

Reid can, I think, rightly be charged with confusion. Part of the trouble is that it is analytic that if F is fundamental or ultimate, then F cannot be explained; explanations come to an end with the fundamental. So, of course, Reid cannot allow that to describe sense perception or to fit it into a lawful scheme or to establish the conditions under which it will or will not occur is to explain sense perception. That would be to give up its ultimate or fundamental character. But this, surely, is to gag at a word. Another source of the trouble is that Reid thinks that to explain is to give necessary connections,[42] and at the same time he recognizes that Hume was entirely right to deny that there are any necessary connections in nature,[43] so that the sorts of things that usually pass for explanations do not pass muster.

Reid is not however, simply confused. His agnosticism is mainly motivated by religious considerations. When Reid says that we cannot explain

42. H 341a.
43. H 481a–84b.

the intellectual powers, he really does not mean that explanations are impossible because our mental powers are in some sense or other ultimates, for he does not really believe that they are. What he really means is that *we* cannot account for such powers as sense perception or memory because ultimately we should have to understand the will of God who made us, and this is beyond us in our present state. The final, and, therefore, the only really genuine explanation of the way things are, for Reid, is the inexplicable will of God. Between God's will and the nature of things in the created world there is a necessary connection, but our intellectual powers in our present state are unable to comprehend it.

4. The Orations contain material, amplified and made more sophisticated in the *Intellectual Powers of Man*,[44] that although in an inchoate form provide the wherewithal for the construction of a theory of mental images that would undercut the notion of ideas as objects in the mind. A rough "rational reconstruction" of this Reidian theory is this: "image" is primarily, i.e. in its literal uses, a word applying to a certain sort of visible thing in the physical world; images are physical things such as representational paintings and sculptures. When we, as we say, have a *mental* image, there is literally no *image* at all involved. We are simply having an experience— a memory experience, an imaginative experience, or perhaps a hallucination—which is like, i.e. similar in certain ways to, the sort of experience we have when we actually see some real thing capable of being represented in or by a real image. Strictly speaking, there is no image at all, although we describe the experience as one of "having a mental image." But the mind is not a *place* for things to be in; the mind has no spatial dimensions as it should have for it to be able literally to contain images. In a perfectly good, but merely grammatical, sense of "in the mind," there are "images in the mind," however, when someone, say, imagines Naples, viz., in the sense that anything is in the mind of which the mind is the *subject*. There is a person who is having an experience *as of the seeing of Naples*, and this experience is, grammatically, "in the mind." But there is no more reason for us to suppose that there must literally be images in the mind when we imagine something than there is to suppose that there must be hands or wombs in the mind in order for us to "comprehend" or "conceive" a thought. This analysis enables us to understand such otherwise unintelligible expressions as "auditory image." Some people are able to imagine "in the mind's ear" tunes and the like, and it is such experiences as of hearing a really sounding tune that underwrite the otherwise odd expression "auditory image," which nobody supposes refers to real but perhaps faint

44. See esp. H 221b, H 254a, H 256b, H 257a, and H 355a.

sounds "in the mind." And so on for other sensory "images," if there are any, pertaining to the other sense modalities.

I must leave it to the judgment of the reader whether this analysis of mental imagery can be cobbled together legitimately out of fragmentary material in Reid's works. I believe it can. And if it is a sound analysis, it is fatal to a theory of ideas-cum-mental imagery as mental objects. The havings of ideas, i.e. mental images, then come to be what common sense takes them to be—degenerate modifications of human experience, the very nature of which presupposes the existence of full-blooded persons moving about and experiencing an objective world of material objects redolent of mind-independent flavors, sounds, colors, shapes. As such, their epistemological interest is considerably diminished.

II

Thomas Reid and the Scottish philosophy of common sense lost their paramount position in the intellectual life of the English-speaking nations around the middle of the last century, and Reid for the most part came to be mentioned, if at all, only in footnotes. There are a number of reasons, some good and some not, why Reid's philosophy fell into disrepute. Kant's judgment of Reid was tremendously influential, and Hegel and all his many philosophical offspring seem to have accepted it almost *in toto*. Also, Reid was incredibly unfortunate in the quality of most of his followers in the Scottish school; their dogmatism and even downright stupidity did Reid no good. Even so, the main fault is Reid's. He simply did not adequately face up to several problems that will always be critical for any philosophy of common sense. For example, despite his explanations of how there can be disputes about first principles among men of equally good judgment, he does not succeed in explaining how a really bang-up, knock-down, self-evident truth could ever be genuinely disputed by a man of sound judgment. To say, as he sometimes does, that doubt or denial of common sense beliefs is an indication of the perversion of judgment by prejudice, miseducation, or worse, seems silly when applied to a man like Hume. Reid also failed to discuss adequately the connections between common sense on an empirical level and metaphysical common sense. Thus, he fails to show how common sense on the metaphysical level can have the pragmatic implications he accuses skeptics of ignoring. Hume's closet skepticism apparently had no effects whatever on Hume's daily intercourse with his companions, although Reid clearly thought it ought to for a consistent Hume; perhaps Reid is right on this matter, but he does not provide us with sufficient reason for thinking so. Reid had a number of other faults as well. He often misunderstands and distorts the position of his opponents in serious ways. He says, to give only one example, that the *cogito* is the sole first principle upon which Descartes sought to build his philosophy. Such blunders did Reid's reputation considerable harm. But all this is not to say that the Scottish philosophy has left no valuable residue that contemporary philosophers might use if they were more familiar with Reid's works. Reid's persistent warnings against the dangers inherent in transgressions against the established structures and usages of language are wholly salutary. And whatever the faults of his commonsense philosophy, Reid was surely right to insist that common sense, although not sacrosanct, is sublime in the richness and fertility of its conceptual scheme and probably will be generally superior to anything a philosopher is likely to think up in his armchair of an afternoon—or even of a lifetime of philosophical afternoons. This is discouraging to those who wantonly fly in the face of common sense, but it ought not to be discouraging to serious and careful philosophers who can be content with real, if modest, gains. Common sense *is* a bit of a spoilsport, but it is incapable of spoiling any philosophical sport that does not deserve spoiling.

I want especially to thank Professor Shirley Darcus Sullivan of the classics department, University of British Columbia, for undertaking the task of translating the Latin of the Philosophical Orations and for tracking down and annotating the more opaque of Reid's allusions. I also want to thank the University of Texas Press for permission to incorporate in this work some material from my article "Reid Redivivus?" which appeared in *Texas Studies in Literature and Language* 14, no. 2 (Summer 1972): 303–12. I want to thank the University of Aberdeen Press for permission to use the W. R. Humphries edition of the Orations in preparing this translation. And I want especially to thank Mrs. Merrily Allanson for preparing the typescript of this work, and Professor Norman Swartz for technical assistance in computer programming.

A Note on the Translation

The Transcription

THIS TRANSLATION OF THE SPEECHES IS BASED ON THE TEXT OF W. R. Humphries, *Philosophical Orations of Thomas Reid* (Aberdeen: Aberdeen University Press, 1937). The transcription has been selectively checked against a photocopy of the original manuscript of the Orations provided by Colin A. McLaren, archivist and keeper of manuscripts for the University of Aberdeen. Humphries notes in his introduction that he regards the manuscript as showing signs of haste. He mentions that Reid fails to loop e's and to dot i's, thus making them sometimes hard to distinguish. Reid also often fails, I noticed, to cross t's.

The Orations give evidence of reworking. Reid makes frequent additions to the speeches in the left and right margins. In some cases, the additions are parallel to the text; in others, they are perpendicular to it. The exact placement of these additions can be in question (as e.g. at the beginning of Oration II). In general, however, the original manuscript presents a very accessible text. It shows a rapid, cursive hand that is usually easy to read.

The text provided by Humphries appears to be a very careful and accurate transcription of the original manuscript. He has given in exact form the capitalization and punctuation used by Reid. In his introduction, he observes that there are two types of errors in the Latin in the original manuscript. The first type includes "slips of the pen" (p. 9). These he corrects. The second includes actual mistakes in the Latin. These Humphries leaves in the text but points out their presence by means of "Sic MS." Humphries also faithfully notes which passages are additions in the margins and whether their placement in the text is clearly indicated or not. He describes in the footnotes any other unusual features of the Latin. On the whole, Humphries appears to have presented accurately the four Orations of Thomas Reid.

This Translation

The four Philosophical Orations of Thomas Reid were never intended by him for publication. This fact helps to explain the occurrence of several mistakes in the Latin of the speeches. The very nature of the Orations— that they were actually delivered—also helped to determine the nature of the Latin used by Reid. The words were arranged in a manner that would ensure that the audience could grasp them easily, and that they would have rhetorical effect.

In the written version, however, the punctuation sometimes marks off by a period words or phrases as though they were a complete sentence. Reid did this also for rhetorical effect, and it would have been clear enough to the audience in the spoken version. But the written version can be confusing because of the occasional ambiguity caused by the punctuation.

In my translation of Humphries' text, I attempt to keep as close to the original Latin as possible. In my footnotes (marked by an asterisk—*), I point out any unusual features of the Latin. In addition, I add notes on some of Reid's allusions that might be obscure to the reader. In the case of the errors in Latin noted by Humphries, I translated the Latin as it would read if it were correct. I have filled out the translation of the Latin only where Reid has written a dangling sentence or has not made quite clear the specific object to which he is referring. As far as possible, I make the translation reflect Reid's Latin in detail.

I should like at this time to express my appreciation for the late Professor G. B. Riddehough's suggestions concerning several difficult points.

—Shirley Darcus Sullivan

ORATION I

Speech delivered in the public auditorium of King's College, Aberdeen April 9, 1753

MY AUDIENCE, IT IS MY PLAN, WITH DUE MODESTY, TO ENTRUST TO your judgment a few observations about the laws of practicing philosophy. And since this is a subject that is generally not treated by philosophers or is touched on only lightly, it is more just, for this reason, for one who is traveling alone through pathless regions, tread on by almost no one before, to request the good faith and indulgence of his learned audience.

In every art and, to be sure, in every activity destined by design and reason for a certain end, it is necessary that there be laws both of the art and of the activity; these laws are sought from the nature and purpose of the art or activity itself and beyond or short of them right, truth, and usefulness cannot exist in that art or activity. It is commonly known that this is the case in arts and operations that are mechanical. That the same holds true in the more elegant arts of painting, carving, architecture, sculpture, and music is agreed upon by those skilled in these arts. Rhetoricians have propounded laws of rhetoric, composition, and pronunciation. Very many men of high repute have been the authors of laws of the art of generalship and of political administration. And although poetry displays divine inspiration, nonetheless at one time Aristotle dared to bind this very subject with laws and to place restrictions on those stimulated by divine frenzy, and after him others did the same, accompanied by the loud applause both of poets and philosophers.

Nay, also the supreme Poet, the Maker of all things and the all-powerful Ruler, while he was establishing the first beginnings of the universe, proposed laws for himself that were in keeping with his wisdom and goodness. And he continues to rule both the material and rational world by the wisest and most favorable laws and the investigation of these laws comprises the principal and most noble part of philosophy.

Since this is the case with respect to these matters, there should not be the smallest doubt that in the case of the art of practicing philosophy, which more than any other art professes that reason is its guide, and which has in view a most noble end, there are no less than in the other arts laws sought from its own nature and purpose. By the norm of these laws, what duly takes place in philosophy ought to take place and by the use of these laws we can judge, amid so many and such different systems of philosophers and methods of practicing philosophy, what has been established legitimately and in accord with the art, what otherwise. Assuredly, it is impossible for philosophy, whose duty it is to reveal the laws both of the other arts and of nature itself, to be itself unfixed, unbound, and lawless.

And in fact, it is surprising that, although in general, laws of the other arts have been established by a common agreement, almost nothing of this type has been made standard in philosophy. From this fact, it is easy to conjecture that, even though philosophy has been thoroughly polished by so numerous and such distinguished men through so many ages, yet it has scarcely at this time left the stage of infancy or at least the stage of adolescence, and that a just measure of the art and its symmetry has not been found. For one can see that the arts do not owe their origin to the laws governing them, but, on the contrary, laws arise from the progress and advanced state of the art itself. In truth, all arts are accustomed to grow little by little from small beginnings until at length, having gained significant increases through the outstanding genius of some individual who has the guidance of nature and a fruitful disposition, they have brought forth surpassing works of art made according to law without law. And finally others, by means of the best and most praiseworthy works of the art, have revealed the laws of this same art; once these laws have been established, true and legitimate works are easily distinguished from spurious ones. And so, from these facts, as we have already stated, a strong indication is given that the state of philosophy is not very advanced, because an agreement has not been reached about the laws of practicing philosophy.

I admit with joy that mathematics (whether you will say it is a part of philosophy or the faithful companion and counselor of it) is free from this failing, since mathematicians agree about the laws of their own art. Naturally enough, they reject and condemn as illegitimate every demonstration of a theorem which is not based on the propositions already proven or on the axioms or common notions set forth by themselves. They reject also every solution of a problem that does not follow from points given or postulated. And so, we recognize that mathematics, based on these few laws, has been cultivated according to law by the ancients and by modern mathematicians, in particular by the most glorious Newton, and that it has taken up increases worthy of the human mind and borne the richest fruits.

As far as philosophy is concerned, however, we find that it was divided by past ages into various schools and sects. Each one of these had a

different method, a different system, of philosophizing about the origin of
the world, the first principles, the order and causes of natural things, about
God, the human soul, the limits of good and evil, the happy life and, in
short, about everything known and unknown, with each school praising its
own views and disparaging those of another. These schools or sects were
generally started by men distinguished for their genius and their art of
speaking; their followers and pupils, led by a blind admiration of their
teacher, dared not advance any further but were slaves to adorning and
cramming full the doctrine handed on to them. Often by their zeal they
weakened and destroyed this teaching. This process went on until at length
someone more daring, who put trust in his own ability, busied himself in
working out new theories and founding a new school or in refashioning
and stirring up an old school that was almost buried.

The hatred and deadly war that arose among the different schools could
only be ended by the destruction of the opposing school, and through the
ages one sect was overthrown by another just as wave is driven back by
wave. And this sport and fierce strife of idle men are thought to be worthy
of the name of philosophy that, by these devices through so many ages,
has grown, to be sure, into a bulk that is enormous, but one of little weight.

Assuredly in so great a heap, a fan is needed in order that the chaff can
be separated from the wheat and given to the winds. Truly, it would be
right to hope that that would occur if an agreement were reached about the
laws of practicing philosophy and to hope not only for this achievement
but also that the inordinate desire for founding schools and sects in philosophy could be bridled and that philosophy could be advanced to a better
and more useful, although not a greater, purpose. We must briefly examine
these questions: how, in truth, precepts and laws of the art of philosophy
can be drawn most successfully from the most outstanding works of the
art, what in particular in philosophy should be established as worthy of the
honor of being a model, and which philosophies have been seen to follow
more closely the legitimate method of practicing philosophy.[1]

Philosophy is divided into three parts by Plato and the Stoics. The first
part deals with life and morals, the second with nature, the third with the
art of carrying on a discussion. Many have treated well the first part that
deals with the topics of life and morals, of baseness and honor, but those
have treated it best who do not expound on these topics with ingenuity and
subtle dialectic, but who strike the minds of men with the importance of
the subject matter and move their hearts. Poets, as well, often achieve this
effect most successfully, and they define what is beautiful and what is base,

1. Cf. H 241a–b.

what is useful and what is not, more fully and better than Chrysippus and Crantor. For this part of philosophy, since it is the most useful part of all and of the greatest importance in relation to the attainment of a good and happy life,[2] by the goodness of God has not been concealed in a secret place nor wrapped in darkness nor sunk in an abyss but has been written by the finger of God on the very hearts of men. And in relation to these subjects, that man philosophizes best who describes and depicts most favorably the internal feelings of an upright man who is struck by a love of virtue. In this type of philosophy, moreover, there have been many famous men, but outstanding, in my judgment, was Socrates of Athens, glory and preeminent ornament of philosophy, not only because of his teaching but also because of his morals; he was the first among philosophers to recall men from an arrogant display of discussing and defining hidden matters and the first to try to induce them to live their lives well. He was almost worthy of the title, Apostle, since his whole doctrine was concerned with the praise of virtue and with summoning men to zeal for virtue and to reverence for the Divine Power. And perhaps it was right for a human being with the guidance of reason to speak fuller or better about the administration of the Divine Power and about the duty of mankind or at least to touch nearer on the truth. Since Socrates wrote nothing, we have received his teaching from Xenophon and, in particular, from Plato. The former appears to hand on the pure and genuine doctrine of his teacher. In the case of Plato, however, there is cause to doubt whether he made Socrates' teaching more elegant with his lofty eloquence or whether he corrupted it with the witty contrivances of his playful genius.

After Socrates and his followers, Plato, Xenophon, Aristotle, Cebes of Thebes[1*] and Aeschines[2*], the Stoics made the best statements about morals; Cicero has set forth most elegantly the teaching of the Stoics in the three books of the *De Officiis*. But those, either among the ancient or the modern writers, who have tried to philosophize about the causes, origin, and nature of virtue more acutely and beyond the common sense of mankind in general, have made little progress and rather have rendered a subject, clear and

2. Cf. H 530–86. Reid shares the common eighteenth-century view of the necessary connection between virtue and happiness.

1*. Cebes of Thebes (fl. fifth century B.C.) was a pupil of Socrates. He appears as an interlocutor in the *Phaedo* and is mentioned in the *Crito* as one of those prepared to help Socrates escape from prison. In ancient times he was reputed to be the author of a Socratic dialogue, the *Pinax*, or *Picture*, depicting happiness as consisting in the practice of virtue.

2*. Aeschines of Sphettus (fl. early fourth century B.C.) was a pupil of Socrates. After the death of Socrates he went to the court of Dionysius of Syracuse. After the expulsion of Dionysius he returned to Athens where he taught philosophy and wrote several dialogues depicting the life and teachings of Socrates. The dialogues are now lost. He is reputed to have been a teacher of Xenocrates.

obvious to the multitude, obscure and doubtful by their philosophical subtleties. In this respect, moreover, Joseph Butler, the Bishop of Durham, is
seen to take the palm.[3]

The chief figures of the Socratic school, Xenophon, Plato, and Aristotle,
have also treated in a distinguished fashion politics, the most noble part of
philosophy, although in this subject as well Plato yielded too much to his
own personality. Among modern philosophers, Machiavelli, Harrington,
and David Hume, who have been taught by the experience of past ages
and by the fate of the governments of both ancient and modern peoples,
have made strong progress in this part of philosophy. The most illustrious
leader, Montesquieu, however, is seen to outstrip all philosophers by a
long distance; he is by nationality a Frenchman, by his character and zeal,
a Briton. This man, instructed by the learning of the whole of history, with
the keenest judgment, with Attic wit, and with Laconic brevity and weight
of diction, has set forth most lucidly the causes, principles, and effects of
laws, morals and politics, from the first beginnings of human nature. From
the British race in particular, he has well deserved the name Briton because
he has taught us, who are blessed with a form of government surpassing
all the governments that either history has shown forth or imagination has
contrived and who are exceedingly fortunate, to recognize our own blessings and to value them highly.

The second part of philosophy is concerned with nature and is called
physics; this must be based on natural history. In this subject, Aristotle,
Theophrastus, and Dioscorides were preeminent among the ancients by
reason of their trustworthiness and diligence, which are especially sought
in this subject; Pliny was also distinguished because of the learning, variety,
and large scope of his undertaking, but he was too credulous and is for
this reason of doubtful reliability.

Francis Bacon[4] outlined with the highest judgment the chief points of
natural history and showed the purpose and usefulness of this subject.
Since, however, a complete and just treatment of natural history would not
be accomplished by the toil of one generation, let alone of one man, it is
to be desired that philosophers more zealously devote their attention to the
task of treating this subject, since from this activity one can hope not only
for many blessings and advantages for human life but also for a more

3. But see H 32b; H 237b; H 350a–b. This sentence is unclear. It seems to damn Butler, but
Reid always had a very high opinion of Butler. The respect in which Butler takes the palm,
therefore, must be that he is among those who make the best statements about morals.

4. Reid always thought of himself as a Baconian. He regarded Newton as having applied and
amplified Baconian principles in physics, and he thought of hmiself as doing the same thing in
the philosophy of mind. See H 11 seq.

natural fruitful progress of natural philosophy that investigates the laws and principles of natural phenomena.

Although almost all ancient philosophers attempted to treat physics, nothing worthy of mention has been handed down by them in this field. All their views are groundless, fictitious, and empty, derived not from legitimate experience with nature but from conjecture and imagination. Deservedly, therefore, is Socrates considered most wise who wittily derided the physics of his own age and preferred to philosophize about these matters not at all rather than factitiously and uselessly. Worthy, in truth, of the highest admiration is Hippocrates of Cos; when philosophers were striving in vain to reach an understanding of the nature of things by conjecture, he alone, taught by a more divine spirit, by means of faithful observation and manifold experimentation, laid the foundations of medicine that were never to be shaken. He alone among the ancients is worthy of the name of natural philosopher, and he should be considered not only the first of the physicians but also one of the greatest philosophers.

The discovery of the magnifying glass rendered the subject matter of natural philosophy greater, since it revealed many objects that were not seen by the naked eye because of distance or small size. By use of the telescope, the movement of the heavenly bodies was observed by Galileo, Hevelius, the Cassinis, father and son, by Huygens and Flamsteed, with trustworthiness, labor, and watchfulness very great, strong, and worthy of kings, and they have opened a way for the establishment of true physical astronomy. This subject the most sagacious Kepler has grasped to some extent, and the leader of geometry and physics, Isaac Newton, has led it to that summit which all gaze at. And this physical astronomy of Newton has been reluctantly accepted by foreign philosophers and not sufficiently understood. At last, it has been illustrated by the *Minimorum Romanorum Commentarium* and confirmed by the recent observations of the most glorious Edmond Halley in particular, of Bradley and those of the French Academy sent to Lapland and Peru, to such an extent that the most stubborn opponents have been compelled to submit.

The supreme genius of Newton, fitted for revealing the laws governing the greatest bodies, has explained reflections of the rays of light, refractions, and color, having detected them by experiments with equal care and acuteness. And in fact, whatever progress in natural philosophy the followers of this mighty man have made, which to be sure is very small, nevertheless whatever this progress is, it is almost all owed to the questions and conjectures proposed by Newton with a modesty singular and worthy of a philosopher.

A few statements must now be made about the art of presenting an argument. Dialectic, which has been used for a long time in schools and was discovered and doubtlessly perfected by Aristotle, reveals the great genius of its author. And perhaps some will think that there is no need for laws of practicing philosophy other than those that dialectic or scholastic logic has proposed about the correct method of reasoning, especially since dialectic for many ages has been taken as the norm of practicing philosophy and as the root and stem of philosophy. Even now, it is considered such by many, and certain people believe that nothing should be thought worthy of the name of philosophy unless it is spring from this plant. Since in truth a plant is known by its fruit, what fruit, I ask, has dialectic borne through so many ages? If it is permitted to speak the truth, one must acknowledge that dialectic has been fruitful of the thorns of controversy and disputation but has been sterile and barren of true knowledge and of inventions useful to mankind. Assuredly in a dispute, a stubborn opponent is sometimes more strongly bound by the fetters of syllogisms, and on that account I believe that syllogistic argument is not completely useless as an instrument of war that it is right for one to employ against an enemy trained with the same skill and arms. If, however, the discussion is carried on with honest men who are lovers of truth or if it is one's purpose to search out the nature, order, and structure of things, we will discover that these arms are useless, burdensome, and annoying. Hear with an impartial mind why I would trust one method or another. First of all, it is certain that the syllogistic method of arguing can be useful in no way unless in the apodeictic type of argumentation, where we arrive at a conclusion by one middle term. Where, however, several arguments or testimonies must either be taken account of or weighed, we consider that it is necessary to lay aside syllogistic reasoning. And therefore, if in any section of philosophy, certainly in mathematics, dialectic ought to bring aid and yet mathematicians, who in everyone's opinion reason in the proper manner, reject the syllogistic pomp and apparatus as a useless hindrance.

Furthermore, one can observe that there are two paths by which the human mind proceeds from things known to things unknown. One is the descent by which the mind journeys from universal propositions to particular points contained in those propositions; the other way is contrary to this and by it an ascent is made from particular points to universal truths. The first way is facile and easy nor in this activity is the mind greatly in need of the help of skill, but on the other hand to recall one's steps, this is the labor, this the task, of the philosopher, since in the nature of things the particular are known first. By means of the senses, experience, testimony, and also by other methods, to ascend in a legitimate manner to the laws and general axioms of nature is in fact to practice philosophy duly and worthily. However, in this journey of ascent, the syllogistic art is completely useless.[5]

And so, since it is evident that the implement of Aristotle is unequal to this task, Francis Bacon, a man of admirable genius, born not only for the advancement but also for the renewal once again of natural philosophy, dared to labor upon the *Novum Organum Scientiarum*. He was the first to teach that natural philosophy is not an offspring of the human mind but a just and lawful interpretation of the works of nature itself or of God.[3*,6] He deservedly should be called a guide to the mysteries of nature, since he unlocked the door of this temple of God and revealed the path to the inner sanctuaries. Nor is there doubt that Newton himself, led by the hand of this preeminent man and taught by his admonitions, brought about in this way successful advances in natural philosophy.

The following are the conclusions drawn from what I have said. Of the art of practicing philosophy, no less than of the other arts, there are laws by which views that are true, genuine, and worthy of the name of philosophy can be distinguished from empty, counterfeit, and illegitimate ones. Although these laws have not yet been formulated by philosophers and have still been less established by common agreement, nonetheless, this achievement is to be expected as the state of philosophy becomes more advanced, and it will result in great profit for philosophy. These laws must be sought from the nature and purpose of philosophy and be illustrated and confirmed by the most approved examples of practicing philosophy. Hip-

5. Reid persisted throughout his life in his erroneous view of syllogistic as a putative "engine of science," which fails in its task of yielding new material knowledge. See H 701–2.

3*. This portion of the text has been expanded in the right-hand margin of the manuscript and this marginal expansion, in turn, has been rewritten at the end of the Oration. A translation of this expanded portion is as follows:

This work (*Novum Organum*) conceived by his mighty mind, he left partly completed, the rest in outline. Nor has anyone up to this time dared to move his hand to the task of finishing the work of so great a craftsman. He was the first to propose one law of practicing philosophy of great importance with which, by this time, the saner philosophers agree, but which scarcely one, with the exception of Newton, has obeyed. The law is that the philosopher is not permitted, as are the poets, to invent tales from his own mind about the nature of things, however probably and consistent these may be, since philosophy is not an offspring of the human mind but a just and lawful interpretation of the works of nature itself or of God. . . . Bacon also was the only one to teach how this true interpretation of nature is to be acquired by relying on experiments and induction by experiments, and on operations in nature or art. So much so is the *Novum Organum* the first and ultimate work of its type that it ought to be called a grammar of nature, or rather the mighty author of that grammar.

6. Cf. H 234–36; H 260–62.

pocrates of Cos, Socrates, Bacon, Montesquieu, and Newton, each in his own type of the art of practicing philosophy, should be considered an Apelles and Praxiteles;[4*] to the work of these men not only the most important points in philosophy but also those especially sound and useful are owed, and on these men he who wishes to describe the laws of practicing philosophy should hold his eyes intent.

My audience, even though I was desirous of trying something of this sort,[5*] since I did not, perchance, weigh sufficiently what strength my shoulders have and what they would refuse to bear, in due course the awareness of my own weakness has persuaded me either to cease from this undertaking or at least to entrust it to renewed thought. The great length of this introduction has given me, who desire it, the opportunity of laying aside for a time a burden unequal to my strength.

And although this task may be arduous, yet it is right for each individual to set forth and carry inquiry into the Republic of Philosophy.

Oration I: Address to the Candidates

Most esteemed candidates, before you are invested according to the solemn rites of the Academy by a decree of the Senate of the Academy, you must be bound by a solemn oath that you will be faithful to Reformed Religion and show gratitude to the Academy, your Alma Mater. Therefore, with your right hands raised, follow me in the prescribed words.

I, in the presence of the omniscient and all-powerful God, vow and swear that I will sincerely profess the doctrine and faith of the Scottish Church (inasmuch as it plainly sets forth teachings taken from the pure word of God), the one and only orthodox church, right to the last breath of my life, standing in strong abhorrence of all heresies of popes and of any others.

Furthermore I solemnly promise that I will generously render support, in as far as I am able, to this Academy, my Alma Mater (to which I owe this training of my mind).

If willingly and knowingly I break this pledge, I do not reject, as my avenger and punisher, God who examines the secret places of the heart, so help me God.

4*. Apelles was a famous Greek painter of the fourth century B.C. Praxiteles was a renowned Greek sculptor of the fourth century B.C.

5*. This portion has been expanded at the bottom of the page in the manuscript. A translation of the passage is as follows: "The most important part of my purpose still remains, namely to propose some examples which I think should be considered to be laws of practicing philosophy; for it is right for each person in a free field to set forth laws for himself. But, my audience, *et cetera*."

I, with the same authority that in bountiful form the highest and most powerful rulers have granted to this University, establish, create, proclaim, and declare you (candidate's name), a Master in the liberal arts and philosophical disciplines. I grant you the power of teaching, writing, deliberating, and of performing all other duties of that type that here or anywhere else are accustomed to be granted to Masters of Arts. And in token of your graduation, I entrust to you this open book and I adorn your head with the cap and I pray to God, thrice the best and the greatest, that the outcome may be successful and fortunate. And I ask that you produce some sample of your ability in the presence of this numerous assembly.[7]

---

7. Reid appends Addresses to the Candidates to all but the last of the Orations. The are all in the same vein. All but this one have been excised.

Oration II

Speech delivered in the public auditorium of King's College, Aberdeen April 28, 1756

ALREADY FROM THIS CHAIR, I HAVE BRIEFLY EXAMINED THE LAWS OF practicing philosophy. Since it is my desire now to pursue the same argument further, hear in summary the chief points of my former discussion; these in truth are comprised as follows. [Of all the liberal arts, there are laws which are to be sought from the nature and purpose of each art; beyond and short of these laws right, truth, and usefulness cannot exist in that art. Therefore, of the art of practicing philosophy as well, which more than all the arts claims reason as its guide, and which has in view a most noble end, there ought to be laws; according to the norm of these laws, what duly takes place, in philosophy ought to take place and by the use of these laws, amid so many systems of philosophers and such different methods of practicing philosophy, we can judge what is established legitimately and in accord with the art, what otherwise. Although such laws have not yet been formulated by philosophers and have still less been established by common agreement, nonetheless, this achievement is to be expected as the state of philosophy becomes more advanced, and it will result in great profit for philosophy. Finally, these laws must be sought from the nature and purpose of philosophy and be demonstrated and confirmed by the most approved examples of practicing philosophy.][1*]

With these points established thus far, the most important part of my purpose remains, namely, with due modesty to propose some very general laws of philosophy by which we can separate philosophy that is true, genuine, and worthy of its name from empty, counterfeit, and illegitimate philosophy. And although the awareness of weakness covers me with blushes as I discuss a topic difficult and almost untreated before—nor, moreover, would I wish it to be thought that this discussion has been ventured on or undertaken by me in an arrogant manner [nonetheless I undertake this

---

1*. The passage within the square brackets is written in the left-hand margin of the manuscript. There is no indication where Reid wished to insert these sentences. Humphries has inserted them here where they seem most appropriate to the context.

task],[2*]since it is certainly right for each individual in a free field to propose laws for himself, nay more, it is an obligation for each person to set forth and carry inquiry into the Republic of Philosophy.

Furthermore, I wish my learned audience to be aware of this point, that it is not my intention to touch on particular laws that are proper to some section of philosophy, although this treatment would be greatly desired. Mathematics certainly rejoices in its own laws derived from ancient times, and therefore, since it was based on a firm foundation, it was refined in a proper manner and it acquired increases worthy of the human mind. Furthermore, Newton, the glory of our race and age, proposed laws appropriate to natural philosophy with the preeminent Bacon showing the way. Thus, it is truly said that we have gained possession of physics as a result of the efforts of these authors in particular. Physics is not an offspring of the human mind, such as were the theories of Aristotle, Telesio, Patrizzi, Gilbert, Descartes and of others that time destroyed along with the other contrived theories of men, but physics has the characteristic of being based on the phenomena of nature that are clearly seen by the eyes and on the laws of philosophy that are established in the very nature of human beings, will remain unshaken through every age, will grow, and be increased, blessing the human race continually with new discoveries.

As far as the other divisions of philosophy are concerned, it does not appear that they have yet attained a state so advanced and fruitful, but we must not despair of this progress, since an agreement will be reached by philosophers on both the general laws of practicing philosophy and the laws appropriate to each section of philosophy. We must now discuss the general laws, either omitting the particular laws or treating them only incidentally and in passing.

And so, in order that no ambiguity can lie concealed in the terminology, one must set forth or demand an explanation of this terminology. Surely, it is the duty of the philosopher, by a correct method of right reasoning, to draw from principles taken from nature itself general conclusions that can be useful to the human race, that can aid the weakness of human life and people in wretched circumstances, and that can in some way elevate the lot of human beings. From this notion of the duty of the philosopher, I undertake to propose and demonstrate general laws of practicing philosophy, few in number to be sure, but of the greatest importance and being in fact widely evident. I ask the indulgence of my learned audience because I am treating a subject almost untouched before.

2*. Since the principal clause in the sentence has been omitted by Reid, I have added the words in the square brackets.

It is, therefore, the purpose of philosophy to improve the human lot and to increase the mastery of man over matter; it is from this fact that we draw the first law of philosophy, namely, that all futile questions and disputes must be removed from philosophy on the grounds that they are unworthy of the name of this art. It cannot be denied, although one is ashamed to admit it, that questions that are often, to be sure, of a subtle nature, but that are either set forth so as to be beyond the understanding of men or empty and of no possible importance for human well-being, have usurped through many ages not only the venerable name of philosophy but also the more holy name of theology. Nor is this surprising, since philosophy, as a result of the barbarism of those ages, was separated from life, the activities of business, and public affairs and was concealed in the monasteries of monks and scholastic theologians and compelled to be a slave to the garrulity of idle men and their itchiness for arguing about subjects of no importance.

Now, however, since more sane and more experienced theologians have learned to purify and cleanse theology, considering those theological disputes and questions to be of small importance that have no influence in promoting virtue and Christian piety, the dirt and rust that was picked up in monasteries through so many dark ages must similarly be wiped away from philosophy, in order that reason can be restored to its splendor, dignity, and usefulness.[1] In this task, we recognize with joy that certain modern philosophers, and in particular our own Bacon and John Locke, have truly met with success through useful labor. [But the too great reverence of antiquity and the inveterate institutions of our ancestors, whether suited to the tyranny and superstition of the Roman Church, to the character of the age, or to the interests of certain parties, did not allow the several philosophical schools to remove these hindrances to philosophy. Therefore, we ought to recognize that we are more fortunate in this Academy and in a few others, and we ought to thank God who is mightiest and best because He, as well as the wisdom of our founder and the character of Reformed Religion, has wished us to practice philosophy freely. Nor are we compelled to give allegiance to Aristotle, Plato, Thomas, or Scotus nor to echo the sentiments of any teacher nor to sell trash and cheap opinions under the name of philosophy.][3*]

True and genuine philosophy, like a good plant, bears good fruit; false and counterfeit philosophy bears either no fruit or bad fruit. And so from

1. Reid's view of medieval philosophy is the standard, albeit mistaken, view common in the eighteenth century. Note also Reid's strong pragmatist tendencies in these passages. Cf. H 268a–b.

3*. The passage within the square brackets appears as an addition in the right-hand margin of the manuscript. It has been rewritten and affixed on an erratum slip to the manuscript at this point in the speech.

its fruit is it known. For this reason, let the philosopher ponder in himself that his art was not established for the arrogant display of arguing about certain matters nor for the indulgence of an inordinate desire for defining matters that are either beyond human comprehension or completely alien to the human lot and role and pertinent in no way to us nor for nourishing controversies nor for defeating an opponent in a dispute. This art was not established for adorning some school or sect in philosophy and for cramming it full with slavish zeal nor for devising a new hypothesis. Those who are eager for these activities and others of this type should be called not philosophers but Sophists, according to ancient custom. Socrates, the wisest of the Greeks, often very wittily derided the arrogance and empty bombast of these Sophists. Dionysius[4*] said that it comprised the words of idle old men for inexperienced youths. Nor should we pass over the very bitter saying of Bacon about such philosophy: this teaching is without a doubt a certain childish form of philosophy, and it has features that are characteristic of children, for it is eager for chattering but weak and immature in relation to accomplishing; it is fruitful of controversies and disputes but unproductive of works.

Far different and loftier is the knowledge that sound philosophy possesses, namely, the knowledge of how to be of advantage to mankind, to prepare true aids for the human mind, to enlarge the mind's inborn strength, to increase the command of man over himself and other things. Sound philosophy knows how to trace out the nature, causes, order, strength, and nexus of things, in order that every art and science that is useful to the human race, with a vital spirit drawn, as it were, from philosophy, might grow and be perfected.

Furthermore, it can be observed that this law I have proposed is useful not only in order that one can know what in philosophy is worthy, as it were, to be retained and what, on the other hand, should be rejected as a useless burden, but also in order that one can judge what is more worthy and more important and what deserves a lower place, since here, as in other matters, one part is more important than another. There are insignificant sections of philosophy; there are also insignificant philosophers. Those men, in truth, must be considered such who spend their life on topics, although not completely useless, yet of smaller value. Just as the author of a dictionary can have a place in the Republic of Letters, even though it is a lower place, in the same way the man who busies himself in gaining

4*. Dionysius, the Tyrant: there were two men, father and son, known as Dionysius, the Tyrant, viz. Dionysius I (c. 430–367 B.C.), and Dionysius II (c. 395–343 B.C.). Both were patrons of the arts and sciences, and both hosted Plato. I have not been able to trace this supposed observation to its source in the literature.

a knowledge of the vocabulary of all flowers, of butterflies, and of snails and the means of destroying them, if he is to be considered a philosopher at all, he must at least be held to be of minor importance.

We propose the following as the second law of practicing philosophy, a law that is closely akin to the first. The philosopher will think that no knowledge, wisdom, or art that is useful to the human race is alien to himself.

One can say with merit and justice that philosophy is not only, as Marcus Tullicus Cicero[5*] states, the mother and parent, as it were, of all praiseworthy arts but also the nurse and nourisher of them. And for this reason, the parent ought to cultivate a holy sharing of duties and a fond fellowship with her offspring; in fact nothing other should be considered of more importance to either of them than this. For we do not fear to assert this fact confidently that there is a no more certain indication of a favorable condition both of the arts and sciences and of philosophy than when the parts are bound together and a fellowship and union come to pass among them. And, on the other hand, we assert that when this communication and union have been disrupted, there follows of necessity a philosophy that is fanatic or useless and sophistic and arts, in truth, that are defective, empiric, and deceptive. Nor would I wish this statement to hold true only in relation to the more liberal arts but also in relation to the mechanical arts and moneymaking pursuits. For there are natural phenomena that belong to each—even of the lowest forms of art, there are, for the most part, individual characteristics that are scarcely found elsewhere—that can be of great use for discovering the causes of things and the forces of nature.

This fact was rightly perceived by Francis Bacon, a most shrewd renewer of philosophy, who for this very reason handed down rules to be followed by the man who wished to be of service to the history of natural philosophy. He taught that the greatest diligence must be applied to comparing the history not only of the natural species but also of the arts both liberal and mechanical, namely agriculture, cattle breeding, dyeing, glassblowing as well as the manufacture of sugar, gunpowder, paper, and products of this sort. Nor should the philosopher pay attention only to those experiments of the arts that pertain to the purpose of his own art but also those experiments that take place in any manner. For example, the fact that uncooked locusts and crabs are of a muddy color, but when they are cooked, they are red, is purely of interest in relation to eating, but is not a useless observation for an inquiry into the nature of redness, since the same phenomenon occurs as well in the baking of bricks. And, therefore, experi-

5*. Cicero, *De Oratore* 1.3.9.

ments of the arts should be gathered and arranged in order, not only so that the individual arts can be more readily perfected, an achievement that should not be considered of small importance, but also, and this is much more important, so that the streams of all experimenters can flow together from all directions into the sea of philosophy and render the philosopher more equipped both for tracing out the causes of things and for discovering inventions useful to the human race. Nay, also in things most common, in things cheap, ignoble, and base, it is not shameful for the philosopher to search out the nature of things. For all things are pure to the pure, and if profit from latrines seemed to have a good smell to the Roman emperor,[6*] much more ought base things to be regarded as a source of light and information. For to bring forth the oracles of nature from all possible objects, whether these give their information freely or whether they must be wrenched by handling and experimentation, is the true practice of philosophy.

Let these statements that have been made concerning the fellowship of philosophy with the common arts suffice. As far as the sciences and liberal arts are concerned, one can observe that these were all regarded in most ancient times as parts of philosophy and, to be sure, as most noble parts. So much was this so that the name of philosophy embraced politics, rhetoric, medicine, poetry, music, and whatever we term by the name of wisdom. These, however, sprouted little by little into different branches and were assigned into separate professions by the appropriate vocabulary, and the common name of the truck was laid aside. Thus, we hear that Hippocrates of Cos was the first to separate medicine from philosophy and to set it up as a distinct profession. Then, as other individuals removed other sections, scarcely anything of greater value was left to philosophy. It is not my intention to start a quarrel about terminology or to condemn the separate professions of the arts and the sciences, since many people can have time for one section, but very few can have time for all. Nonetheless, we believe that this separation has resulted in a great loss to the liberal arts and sciences and is a disgrace for philosophy, because by the injury either of men or of time, through very many ages, these arts and sciences, just like most noble and exceedingly productive branches, have been cut off from philosophy and set up, as it were, by their own roots. Not only has the name of their parent and nourisher been rejected, which would be of small importance, but the link and compact has been broken. From this cause it happens that these arts and sciences, deprived of their

6*. The emperor Vespasian (A.D. 9–79) placed a tax on public latrines. When his son found fault with him for placing this tax, he remarked that money had no smell. See Suetonius, *Divus Vespasianus* 23.3.

native blood and juice, have been seen to decline and become weak. Moreover, philosophy has been robbed of its most noble branches and left with tender shoots, a scornful trunk, a useless piece of wood, busying itself with covering its own nakedness with its barren twigs. In not many years hence, everyone who is moderately versed in the history of philosophy will be aware that it has been reduced to this state. How rightly, therefore, has someone complained: "Galen brings help, Justinian, honors/But we philosophers are a wretched little mob."

And in fact, that type of philosophy that is not of service to the administration of the state, rhetoric, medicine, the art of war, the art of sailing, or commerce is a ridiculous object that ought to be left to monks and idle men because, inasmuch as it is useless, it cannot possibly be held in honor and esteem for a long time, nor ought it to. True philosophy is connected with all the sciences and liberal arts and contains in itself the elements of all of them; it nourishes them all and joins with them in a mutual compact.

By the third laws of practicing philosophy, the philosopher is forbidden to play the role of the poet or to invade the sacred privileges of the bards.[2] Poets have always been permitted to compose whatever they pleased, provided they could devise a certain probability for their tales and bring about a harmony of the parts. And so, let the apt weaving of tales be the proper characteristic of poets but let it be a sacrilege for a philosopher to claim this practice for himself. Whatever is accomplished and contrived by the strengths of the human mind, we wish to be called poetry, not philosophy, and we leave it to those who have dreamed on Parnassus with its double peaks.[7*] For the duty of the philosopher is a far different one, namely, to interpret in a pure fashion the works of God, the supreme Poet, and not to corrupt these works by any intermingling of the offspring of the human mind. This restriction, to be sure, is very disagreeable to the pride and arrogance of mortal man who prefers to command things rather than to obey them and to cut through the knots of nature by the force of his mind rather than to untangle them by a careful and painstaking process. And so, the mind of men is easily carried away to a certain divination and augury about the nature of things on the basis of trivial conjecture. The human mind, however, is hostile and averse to gaining an understanding of the language of things themselves and to interpreting their meaning, as a more humble task. For all the works of God have a certain meaning and speech;

2. Cf. H 99b. Hamilton notes that Hume, Reid, and Kant all hold the same doctrine of the incompatibility of creative imagination and philosophical talent.

7*. This reference to Parnassus is taken from Persius, *Prologus ad Saturas*, line 2: "in bicipiti somniasse Parnasso/to have dreamed on Parnassus with its double peaks." This same reference occurs in the fourth Oration of Reid.

they speak not to the ears but to the mind. Assuredly, with a voice that is profound and intelligible to all, they announce the power, wisdom, and goodness of their Founder. But also with a gentle voice and a language that is not vernacular, but one that can be understood with zeal and effort, they reveal what they are, by what law they were founded by their most wise Author, with what strength they have been endowed, by what bond they are joined among themselves and finally by what work, by which duties, they can aid mankind. To fashion a grammar of this language, to understand the words, to note the analogy in order that we can at last grasp its meaning, is the task, not of uncertain conjecture, but of legitimate explanation. To accomplish this task is the true role of a philosopher. The preeminent Bacon, who was the most successful of mortals in defining objects, was never more successful than when he stated that philosophy is an interpretation of nature, nor as I believe, could the force and nature of philosophy be grasped with a more suitable definition. Just as it is the duty of the Christian theologian to draw forth from the pure word of God the dogmas of religion and not to add anything derived from his own or some other person's thought, in the same way it is the duty of the philosopher to reject all the divinations and contrivances of men as apocrypha and to embrace this object alone, sound and divine, as it were, namely, what the works of God say and relate. And, nonetheless, for the majority of philosophers, both ancient and modern, this practice has almost been the rule, namely, after gazing upon objects and examples for a short time or conducting a few experiments, to devise causes, an order and interconnection that suit the phenomena to some extent, and they wish this practice to be considered the method of practicing philosophy. Nothing, however, is more alien to philosophy. Let it be divination, let it be augury, let it be thought based on preconceived notions, or anything else that is of little value; it certainly is not philosophy.[3]

If in reality these statements are true, in so great a mass of philosophical writings, how little there is that ought to appear worthy of the name! Among so many names of philosophers a faithful interpreter of nature is, to be sure, a rare bird upon the earth.[8*] Nonetheless, among the ancients, we believe that Hippocrates of Cos, the first of the doctors, was especially worthy of honor, who handed on to his disciples the precepts of his art, derived in a pure fashion from observations and experiments, with hy-

---

3. Cf. H 200a; H 472b. Actually, the language in which Reid states the nature of scientific explanation derives almost as much from Berkeley as from Bacon. See Berkeley's *A New Theory of Vision*, secs. 144, 147, and *Principles of Human Knowledge*, secs. 66, 108.

8*. This reference to the "rare bird" is taken from Juvenal, *Satura* 2.6.165: "rara avis in terris nigroque simillima cynco/ a rare bird on earth and most like a black swan".

potheses rejected, and taught them to tread in the same footsteps. Second, we deem Socrates of Athens, glory of philosophy, and scourge of the Sophists of his own era, worthy of honor. He in matters pertaining to virtue, morals, and the duty of man closely followed nature as a guide, but in unknown subjects, he was both quick to confess frankly his own ignorance and was prepared to reveal the ignorance of the sciolists.

Among modern philosophers, the mighty intellect of Bacon first taught that philosophy is the interpretation of nature; he demonstrated this most lucidly in an outstanding work called the *Novum Organum Scientiarum*, and he partly set forth the rules of this interpretation. At last, after the course of a long time, the throng of philosophers appears to agree reluctantly with this man. Scarcely one, however, will you find, with the exception of Newton, who at some time does not slip back furtively into fictitious hypotheses.

By the fourth law, we wish care to be taken that the philosopher does not busy himself in overthrowing common notions, unless he wishes to render himself and his art a public object of derision.[4] For there are not only in mathematics but in all human activities axioms or common notions, known alike to the learned and the unlearned, to philosophers and laymen, that snatch up assent from the very constitution of human nature; in accordance with these axioms every principle of life revolves. If these common notions were removed, human plans, just like the dreams of a sick man, could have neither measure nor end and everything would of necessity be turned upside down. These common notions are both more ancient and more stable than the whole of philosophy; they have their deep roots fixed in human nature. So true is this that to tear these away by philosophical devices would be an insane and empty undertaking. For either these are true and certain, or the whole life of man is a dream and a fit of madness. And assuredly, philosophical subtlety will always furnish a ridiculous spectacle to all who have a sane mind, when it is compared with the common sense of men. Who, therefore, would wish, like Zeno, to prove that motion is impossible? Who maintains with Hobbes that there is no natural distinction between what is base and what is honorable? Who asserts with David Hume that no trust should be placed in the senses, memory, in testimony or proof or who can believe that this world had a beginning entirely without cause? I say that the man who attempts to support these and other such monstrosities of opinions with empty subtlety ought not to be thought to

4. It is impossible to list all the related passages in Reid's *Works* in connection with Reid's remarks from here to the conclusion of Oration II; there are too many. Some of the more important references are (Essay 6, "Of Judgment,") H 413–475; H 108b; H 209a–b; H 230b; H 329b; H 637–40.

practice philosophy but either to be playing a game or to be mad. Whoever enters a contest against the common sense of men will discover that he has come upon an adversary who is vigorous, nay rather invincible, to whom in the end he will have to surrender, since no one will depart from such a contest as a victor, no one without disgrace.

Finally, we wish philosophy not only to refrain from opposing common notions but also to be erected and built upon them. All legitimate reasoning must follow from principles that are given and granted. Mathematicians who have well grasped this principle first of all set forth axioms, the basis and foundation, as it were, of their whole science; if these are removed, the science collapses, but if they are established, it remains unshaken, a mighty structure, the glory of the human mind, striking the stars with its lofty head.[9*] This principle, which has been upheld in mathematics for a long time by the agreement of all, the preeminent Newton first dared to apply to physical astronomy, namely, by building this subject on three or four common notions that he called the rules of practicing philosophy. These rules, known to all who have sampled Newton's philosophy, are axioms, pertaining not to mathematics but to physics, and on these axioms and the phenomena perceived by the senses, on two columns of solid adamant as it were, rests whatever is found in the physics of this man that is sensible and sound. Thus, in every part of philosophy, there are certain first principles, resembling most closely the common sense of man, on which the rest lean with their whole weight, and these principles are so closely joined together that the statement that Cicero[10*] once made about geometry can be applied to all the other parts of philosophy as well, namely, that if the first principles are given, all the others must follow. And just as the axioms of Euclid are sufficient to support the whole of mathematics, so Newton's rules of practicing philosophy, if I am not mistaken, will be sufficient for the whole of physics, nor will there ever be need of other rules. But as far as phenomena are concerned, the diligence of men will always furnish new information, grasped by observation and experiments, from which physics, now supported on a firm foundation and daily increased by new reinforcements, will continue to raise its head on high. Moreover, what has been established first in mathematics, then in physics, to the great advantage of these sciences and of the human race, we hope will be established in the other parts of philosophy as well, that is, that they will be built in an orderly fashion upon common notions and phenomena. Nor have I, as I repeatedly turned over this problem in my mind,

9*. This expression is taken from Horace, *Carmina* I. 1.36: "sublimi feriam sidera vertice/I shall strike the stars with my lofty head."

10*. Cicero, *De Finibus* 5.83.

found any cause that would make this hope impossible. For there are axioms and phenomena in ethics and politics, no less than in physics, on which all right reasoning in these sciences depends. What, therefore, prevents these parts of philosophy as well from acquiring a true and legitimate form of knowledge by which they can unravel, just as if with the thread of Ariadne, their winding paths and labyrinths and advance further by a correct and definite path to their topmost peaks?

My audience, I have dared, relying on your indulgence, to set forth these points about the general laws of philosophy and I entrust them to your judgment; if you know of any more correct view, candidly impart it: if you do not, make use of these laws as I do.

ORATION III

1759

IT IS MY INTENTION AT THIS TIME TO SET FORTH A FEW OBSERVATIONS about the human intellect and its primary and most simple operations and to entrust them to the judgment and good faith of this learned assembly.

Formerly, I suspected, but now I know for certain, that the philosophy of the human intellect, even though it has been subjected to study by excellent minds in this generation and in the previous century, has yet right up to the present time been enveloped in darkness and based on hypotheses and fancies of the human mind rather than on an accurate analysis of the operations of the intellect. Why I hold this opinion will become clear in part from what I shall say; in the meantime, it is known by all who are moderately versed in this type of philosophy that dogmas have everywhere been accepted about ideas, judgment, and apprehension, not only bound together by knotty subtleties, but also often contradictory and in strong opposition to the common sense of men and more favorable to the theory of acatalepsy of the Skeptics than to sane and useful knowledge.[1]

For this reason, without doubt, it has happened that prudent men generally have little knowledge of abstract questions and disputes, which are commonly called metaphysics and which depend on the philosophy of the human mind, because neither do they expect any fruit to result from these disputes nor do they hope for a solution of them. Nay more, it has been discovered by experience that the most brilliant men who have more subtly traced out the operations of the intellect generally either have become skeptics or have woven threads suitable to the teachings of skeptics.

From these indications, no small suspicion should arise that the state of this part of philosophy is not a happy one. And, therefore, axioms that have been put forth about ideas, judgment, and apprehension, even though they have been regarded as certain by philosophers, should not be rashly accepted. These axioms should be subjected again to an accurate exami-

1. See esp. H 97–99; H 201–11; H 238–42.

nation lest anything false or doubtful has worked its way into them that could cause difficulty for the man who is desirous of truth and, just like a will-o'-the-wisp, lead him astray into the sterile and disagreeable wilderness of scepticism.

By the term apprehension, philosophers understand the bare concept of anything without any affirmation or denial.[2] Apprehensions are often expressed by one or several words, as, for example, "sea," "tranquil sea," "a very high mountain, rough with rocks and covered in snow," and similar word groups that, since they neither affirm nor deny anything, are not called propositions but terms either simple or compound in composition. That operation of the intellect, however, which is expressed in words containing some affirmation or denial is called judgment. And so the phrase "a wise man" is a term indicating a simple apprehension, but the phrase "a wise man is he who speaks little" is a proposition, a sign of judgment.

Just as an apprehension is often expressed in several words, so a judgment is often expressed in one word, especially in the Greek and Latin languages.[3] And so, the words *diruit* (he scatters), *aedificat* (he builds), *mutat* (it changes), are three propositions expressed in three words. Nonetheless, we must note that not only terms but also propositions can be simply apprehended without the operation of judgment. For there is no one even from the common mass of people who does not know that to understand or to apprehend some proposition is one thing, but it is another thing to make a judgment of that proposition and believe it is true or false. Therefore "to apprehend" is the same as to understand, to conceive, and to imagine, but "to judge" is to agree or disagree, to know, to believe, or to hold an opinion.

To this point, philosophers are seen to proceed with sufficient caution, with clearness, and without stumbling. Nor are those who do not set forth a logical definition of apprehension and judgment to be blamed, but rather those who have dared to define with a logical definition the activities and simple faculties of the mind. For just as definition is not suited to whiteness, extension, duration, and similar qualities that are entirely lacking in composition, and if we should wish to explain what these words mean to someone who did not know, we would have to use synonyms or periphrases or a demonstration of what we meant to the eyes or to the mind, the very same must be said about apprehension and judgment, nay also about reasoning as well. Diverse and different are the activities and faculties of the mind and each is of its own kind. Just as a blind man could never under-

2. Cf. H 223a–b; H 360–68.
3. Cf. H 413–21; H 426–34.

stand the nature of whiteness from any definition, so no one could ever understand the nature of apprehension, judgment, and reasoning who is not endowed with all these faculties and is not aware in himself of their operations. For although judgment is defined by apprehensions, it does not follow from this that judgment is composed in any way of apprehension or that it is a modification of apprehension, as some philosophers contend.[4] Also, although reasoning cannot exist without judgment, nevertheless reasoning or logical inference is not composed of judgments, nor is it a modification of judgments but something of a different kind. For to believe and to reckon, to agree to a proposition and to draw one proposition from another, are without doubt not identical, nor are they operations of the same kind. One can illustrate the distinction between the operations of the intellect by a parallel drawn from a very familiar object, namely, the extension of bodies. We know there are three types of extension, namely, line, surface, and solid. Surface is defined by lines and yet is not a modification line, nor does any ratio exist between surface and line. Solid is defined by surfaces and yet is not a modification of surface but a different type of extension. In a similar fashion do the three operations of the intellect exist.

And so, we wish this view to be held, namely, that apprehension, judgment, and reasoning are three entirely different operations of the human intellect, each of its own kind no less than smell, taste, and hearing, and that the nature of these operations and the difference between them are not to be explained by logical definition but to be grasped by an awareness of the operations themselves.

And these points must be noted all the more for this reason that philosophers are seen either not to have sufficiently paid attention to them or to have held an entirely different opinion. John Locke, a man who has served both philosophy and the human race extremely well, intimated, not without a certain boastfulness that is to be condoned in discovers, that he was the first to demonstrate that nature of judgment, and that no one before him had given a definition of this faculty about which both philosophers and laymen speak everyday.

The name and authority of Locke, to be sure, carry great weight with me, but I fear that this most shrewd man has rendered this faculty of the mind more obscure by his definition and has given occasion for many errors to arise. All of us know correctly and clearly what judgment is, if an inquiry is not made into its nature, but if one does seek to discover its nature, even philosophers are at a loss. This holds true for all simple things

---

4. Reid refers here to Hume. See *Treatise of Human Nature* 2.3.7. 94–98, Selby-Bigge edition.

of an individual kind, and so it should be. For since all definition is based on the genus and species of the object defined, there can be no definition of a genus itself unless it is a species of some more complicated or more simple genus.

However, let us hear the views of this philosopher on the nature of judgment. It is, he says, a perception of the agreement (suitability) or disagreement (discordance) of ideas.[5] Here, we must seek what he means by perception, for it must signify here either the simple apprehension or the judgment of the suitability of ideas. If, however, perception signifies apprehension, it then follows that judgment is a form (species) or modification of apprehension, a view that is in opposition to the common sense of men, nor is this view anywhere asserted by this philosopher in his published works.

If, however, perception does signify judgment, this definition smacks very little of the extreme accuracy of Locke, for he would never have made the statement that judgment is the judgment about the agreement or disagreement of ideas. Hence, unless I am mistaken, it is sufficiently clear either that this most brilliant man supposed that judgment was a form of simple apprehension or that he certainly had not sufficiently discerned that these operations are of an entirely different type.

Later, we will discuss Locke's views about ideas; in the meantime, one can note that it seems surprising that a man who was so keen sighted did not realize that, according to his system, we can make judgments not only about the agreement or disagreement of ideas but also about many other matters, as, for example, about the existence both of ideas and of the objects of which the ideas are images, about the agreement or disagreement of things with the ideas by which ideas are declared by him to be either true or false.

This philosopher elsewhere correctly observes that there are many things that cannot be defined, and he rightly criticizes the definition of time or duration given by Aristotle.[6] I fear that the definition of judgment given by Locke is liable to the same censure.

Hume, a more recent and more bold philosopher, outstanding for his metaphysical acuteness and his genius, in his *Treatise of Human Nature* and in his philosophical essays learnedly teaches that judgment is nothing other than a strong and vivid apprehension.[7] He boldly asserts in his own

5. Reid is simply wrong here; this is how Locke defines "Knowledge." See *Essay Concerning Human Understanding*, bk. 4, chap. 14. But Reid was not so careless in his published work; cf. H 415; H 426.
6. Locke, *Essay*, bk. 2, chap. 14.
7. Hume, *Treatise* 1.3.7; 3.1.1. See H 358a–59b; H 107a.

manner that sensation, imagination, memory, belief or conviction, because they have the same object, are the same and differ among themselves only by degree. Thus, to believe the tales of Aesop is simply to have a strong and vivid idea of them, but to understand and not believe these tales is to have a weak and feeble idea of them. If you ask, my audience, by which argument this philosophical madness is supported, here you shall have it. He says that the man who believes the tales has the exact same ideas in his mind as the man who only understands them. In no way, therefore, do understanding and believing differ between themselves except that, while we believe, the ideas are more vivid, but while we understand, they are more weak. I am surprised that the philosopher stopped here. His argument leads us further in the following way. The man who believes a story is true has the same ideas as the man who believes it is false and, therefore, to believe something is true and to believe it is false are the same thing; they differ, in fact, only by degree in proportion as the ideas are stronger or weaker. And here certainly this philosopher ought to have taught us whether the ideas of some proposition are stronger when it is believed to be true or when it is thought to be false. Assuredly it is difficult to refute such monstrosities of opinions in a serious manner.

If anyone had said that motion was a degree of size, he would have been ridiculed, not refuted, nor does that man seem to me to speak any less absurdly who asserts that judgment is a degree of apprehension. And so, in a matter that is so obvious, it is sufficient to observe this point alone: the human mind in relation to the same object can employ faculties or activities that are entirely different. Of anger and love, of the intellect and the will, the object can be the same, but, nonetheless, it does not follow that anger is a degree of love or that the will is a degree of the intellect. In the same, way we can either conceive of a proposition simply or make a judgment about that same proposition, whether it is true or false, doubtful or certain, useful or useless. No less distinctly and clearly are these two operations separated that the intellect is distinguished from the will or hearing from smell.

Let these statements suffice about the distinction of apprehension from judgment, a topic, to be sure that would be sufficiently clear and easy to grasp, if it had not been covered with philosophical dust and entangled with spider's web.

The throng of philosophers teaches that simple apprehension is of three kinds, namely, sensation, imagination, and pure intellect. I suspect, however, that this division is not accurate nor sought from the nature of the subject. For first of all, even though what philosophers mean by sensation is perchance sufficiently well understood, namely, those operations of the mind that are brought into being with the external senses playing a middle role, the senses being sight, hearing, and the rest, nevertheless, I think that these operations are judgments rather than simple apprehensions. I am not able to observe this learned assembly with my eyes without also believing in its presence and being overcome with modesty. The senses are witnesses of things; we understand their testimony with nature as our interpreter, and by the same guidance of nature, we provide a most firm assent to this testimony. By the same method, we grasp a sensible object and we believe that it exists because the senses witness to its existence, and we rely on no other argument than sensation itself. In every sensation, therefore, the apprehension is not simple but joined with judgment and belief. From these observations one can note how little the teaching of almost all philosophers is in accord with nature, since they teach that simple apprehension is the first operation of the intellect, and that the mind then joins together its own apprehensions and compares them in turn with themselves, and from this action judgments result. In truth, although this operation is simplest, yet it is not primary. For since sensation is prior to imagination, it will follow from such statements that judgment is prior to simple apprehension. We do not, therefore, form judgments from simple apprehensions by putting the apprehensions together. Rather, it must be said that simple apprehensions are formed from natural judgments through analysis or resolution. The process is no different from that which occurs in the case of natural bodies; these are composed of salt, water, earth, and other simple elements, but nature does not display these elements to us in a separated form, late to be put together by skill, but exhibits them mixed and arranged in compound bodies, to be separated by skill and chemical analysis.[8]

As far as imagination and pure intellect are concerned, these have been separated by philosophers in such a way that in imagination there is a phantasm or image of a thing in the brain, but in pure intellect there is no such image. It is clear that this distinction is based on pure hypothesis. For who, I ask, knows that there are phantasms of things in the brain? Who has ever shown by an argument that is either certain or even probable that such phantasms exist?

Dismissing, therefore, this division on the grounds that it is insufficiently accurate and based on an empty hypothesis, I pass to the doctrine of philosophers on the nature and manner of apprehension.

There is an old belief accepted, as far as I know, by all ancient and modern philosophers, namely, that the human mind does not immediately perceive objects that are external and absent but perceives them through

8. Cf. H 107a; H 376a; H 396–98.

certain images or likenesses depicted in the mind that are called ideas. Whatever men think, about whatever thing they reason or pass judgment, these philosophers contend that ideas existing in the mind itself are the immediate and nearest object of thought. Plato asserts that ideas of all things have existed in the Divine Mind from eternity. Malebranche, a most shrewd philosopher, and his followers maintain that we perceive all things in God by contemplating the ideas in the Divine Mind in as far as God wishes to reveal them to us. The rest of the philosophers believe that the ideas by which we perceive things exist in the human mind itself. All Platonists, Peripatetics, and Cartesians, Malebranche, Locke, Berkeley, and Hume agree that no perception is possible without ideas. This doctrine of ideas, set forth by modern philosophers theorizing about the human intellect, could fill one page as well as another. With great effort, men have disputed whether these ideas are inborn or acquired by sensation and reflection, whether abstract and general ideas are given, or whether, in truth, all ideas are of a single nature. Many views have been handed on about ideas that are clear and obscure, distinct and confused, adequate and inadequate, true and false, simple and compound, real and imaginary. All judgment, all knowledge, and reasoning are taught to be nothing other than the comparison of ideas and the perception of the relationships between them. Words are taught to be symbols not of things but of ideas,[9] and finally it has reached this point (nor should this give cause for wonder) that men, even of high esteem among philosophers, maintain that there is nothing else in the nature of things except ideas.

In so loud a din about ideas, to question their existence will seem perhaps to some to be a bold and rash undertaking. Since, however, this doctrine is entirely a personal possession of philosophers and completely unknown to men of sane mind who have never been imbued with philosophy, nay more, since it is completely paradoxical and alien to the common sense of mankind in general, I believe that it is not unlawful nor unfitting for a philosopher to examine the following questions discreetly with the modesty due to the authority of philosophy: what is the nature of this doctrine, what was its origin, on what basis is it supported, and to what conclusions does it lead us?

Of those things that are observed with the mind, certain are present in the mind itself, such as thought, desire, affection, and other operations of the mind; others, however, exist outside the mind, such as the sun, moon, the wandering and fixed stars, and whatever in the nature of things is known to us and is outside of ourselves, namely, outside the mind itself and its

9. See H 117b–18a for Reid's criticism of Locke's semiotic.

operations and accidents.[10] The human mind embraces not only things that actually exist, whether outside of us or in the mind itself, but also many objects that do not exist at the present time, namely, things that have passed away and things that will exist in the future, nay also possibilities that neither exist nor have ever existed are sometimes observed by the mind, such as a golden mountain or a sea of milk. Ancient philosophers have justly said that the mind, endowed with so many and such great powers, is a particle of Divine Breath, born of God and related to him. Those, however, who practice dialectic have not thought it to be sufficient to praise and wonder at these powers of the human spirit, but have thought it to be their duty to render an account of them and to work out some explanation of the phenomena of the intellect. Hence, the theory of ideas was born. And so, they assume that this point is granted and conceded, namely, that the mind by its very nature is endowed with an awareness of its own operations, so much so that it can perceive whatever is in itself; they maintain that these operations are assuredly nothing other than modifications of the mind itself of which by its very nature it must be conscious. To determine, in truth, in what way the mind can embrace or perceive external objects that are separated, perchance by a long distance, and also those that have passed away and do not exist now is a difficulty; this is a knot worthy of a conqueror, and it was for the sake of loosening this knot that the ideas were invented and accepted with strong agreement right from the age of Plato. For in this way, all perception is resolved into consciousness, since we can be aware of ideas that exist in the mind and that represent all external objects.

It was the opinion of Aristotle and the Peripatetics that all things that exist in the world always send forth intelligible forms (species) of themselves and that these forms are imprinted on the passive intellect and retained by it; these forms are the ideas that the mind uses to perceive external objects. Modern philosophers, however, with the celebrated Descartes as their leader and teacher, have rejected the view that intelligible forms are sent forth from things, believing this to be a fictitious hypothesis. Nonetheless, they believe that ideas must be held in the mind on the grounds that they are necessary in all perception and memory. And the whole philosophy of the human intellect handed down by Descartes, Malebranche, Locke, Berkeley, David Hume, and Henry Home is based on these ideas.[11]

Since, however, in philosophical matters not the authorities but the theories must be weighed, one must, in spite of such great names, subject

10. Cf. H 221–22 on the internal/external distinction.
11. See H 262–310 for Reid's detailed account of the history of the theory of ideas.

this hypothesis of ideas to a more accurate examination. For this reason, such an examination is more necessary because this hypothesis appears to have been accepted as a result of philosophical authority and tradition rather than to have been established by solid proofs.

And so, *first* of all, since this doctrine of ideas has been invented in order that the phenomena of perception and memory could be more easily explained, one must note that there are very many phenomena of nature that the weakness of the human mind is incapable of explaining, nay more, will always be incapable of explaining.

To give an account of a phenomenon is simply to demonstrate that such a phenomenon is in accord with some known law of nature.[12] Of the laws of nature themselves, however, no explanation can be given except that they are the will of the supreme Founder of all things. And so, in the material world, no account or physical causes can be given to explain why every body has extension, is impenetrable, inert, and movable; we must be content with this fact alone that the Founder of things has wished this to be the nature of bodies. Whoever will attempt to give an account of these phenomena will not increase philosophy but will confound it with empty hypotheses.

Thus, in a similar manner, there are many activities relating to the human mind of which we will try only in vain to render an account. How the mind thinks, in what way it is conscious of its thoughts and operations, completely escapes us. By no hypothesis shall we be able to explain or to give an account of these faculties. Surely, therefore, the same statement must be made about the perception of external things and the memory of objects that have passed away. Surely these faculties are, in truth, primary and simple, not composed of, nor to be reduced to, other faculties but implanted in our minds by God who is mightiest and best and to be exercised according to the laws and within the limits established by him. For in the mind, no less than in the material world, there are first principles of which no explanation can be given; there are other secondary principles that have arisen from and are bound with the first principles and that are to be brought to light by analysis.[13] The doctrine of ideas maintains without any manifest proof that perception and memory are not primary faculties but have their origin from another faculty, namely, from the consciousness of the ideas that are present in the mind itself. This doctrine alleges, without any manifest proof, that every man shut in, as it were, in a *camera obscura* perceives nothing outside but only the images or ideas of things depicted

12. Cf. H 54b–60a; H 260b–62a; H 234a–42a.
13. Cf. H 434–68.

in his own *camera*. This theory also maintains that the ideas or images of things that are external and have passed away exist in the mind, a theory that is not proven by any argument. One should not, therefore, rashly place his trust in such hypotheses, especially since they are so adverse to the common sense of mankind.

In fact, saner philosophers now recognize that the phenomena of nature must be explained not by hypotheses but by facts known from experience with the laws of nature. And, although it has been customary for both ancient and modern philosophers to devise from their own minds hypotheses that suit phenomena to some extent and to sell these in the name of philosophy, yet nothing is more alien to true philosophy. This is to practice divination, not philosophy.

The intelligible forms of the Peripatetics and ideas imprinted on minds are parts of this same hypothesis, which rest on the same foundation and are joined to themselves by a binding compact. With what right, therefore, and with what injury Descartes and his modern followers have dismissed and rejected on part of this hypothesis and retained the other, let themselves observe.

Second, we must inquire whether, if the theory of ideas is granted, perception and memory are appropriately accounted for and explained by this theory. The following is the knot that must be untied: in what way can the mind perceive external bodies, separated perchance by a long distance, nay also bodies that have passed out of existence? The philosopher says that this happens as follows. There are ideas present in the mind, representations of things that are external or have passed away; the mind, conscious of these ideas, perceives things that are external and have passed away with the ideas playing a middle role. Now, granted that there are ideas of things in the mind of which the mind is conscious, by what skill or by what indications, I ask, can the mind either know or even portend that these ideas are representations of other things?

I review in my mind in how many ways one thing could represent another, whether as a substitute, as an image or effigy, or as a symbol, but I meet with no success. Sometimes, I conceive of ideas as being an interchange for things and playing a role, but I look for their credentials, and nowhere do I find compelling documents. Sometimes, I conceive of ideas as images or effigies of things, but then, in truth, the difficulties are increased both in number and in size, since there are many existences of which no image or likeness can be conceived. What would be the image of sound or taste or smell, I should like philosophers to state.

As far as those things are concerned that have shape, extension, and color, I can easily conceive of images of these painted in a picture, but by what skill they can be painted on the mind, which is without extension and immaterial, goes beyond my understanding.[14]

If, finally, I allege with Aristotle that there is a certain passive intellect in which, just as in a *camera obscura*, images are received, I am still pressed by a most grievous difficulty. For by what divination could I be taught that these images painted in my *camera obscura* are representations? How am I to be taught that the forms present and imprinted on my mind represent things that are external or that have passed out of existence? In fact this hypothesis of ideas does not loose the knot but twists together several others that are most difficult.

Finally, let us suppose that ideas represent things like symbols; in this way, words and writing are known to express everything. Let the intellect, therefore, be instructed by ideas, not in the manner of a *camera obscura* with painted images but like a written or printed book, teaching us many things that are external, that have passed away, and that will come to be. This view does not solve the problem; for who will interpret this book for us? If you show a book to a savage who has never heard of the use of letters, he will not know the letters are symbols, much less what they signify. If you address someone in a foreign language, perhaps your words are symbols as far as you are concerned, but they mean nothing to him. Symbols without interpretation have no value. And so, if ideas were symbols of things, the art of interpreting ideas, in truth, would be the beginning and source of human wisdom, and yet about such an art neither philosophers nor grammarians nor critics nor lawyers, no not even the interpreters of dreams, have ever dreamed. From what I have said, if I am not mistaken, it is clear that the hypothesis of ideas increases the difficulties of perception and memory and in no way diminishes them, and for this reason, it is scarcely suitable for an explanation or elucidation of the phenomena of these faculties.

Although approval may be given to those who assert that ideas exist, yet, one must note that no indication or trace of them appears to me as I carry out this investigation in a serious manner.

I remember that I heard from a distance a rather large bell tolling the half hour. If it had never been my lot to be educated in philosophy, without doubt I would have believed that the very sound of the bell that had passed away and was no longer in existence was observed immediately by my mind, nor would I have thought that I needed some intermediate (mediate) object or idea by which the sound that had departed could be represented

---

14. Cf. Reid's strictures on "image" in H 305; H 224–25.

to my mind, as long as I was endowed with memory. But philosophers teach me that a thing that has passed away cannot be observed by my mind immediately or by itself, but that there is an idea or image of the sound present within my mind that the mind contemplates immediately and that represents the sound that has passed away. Let us ponder for a while what this image of a sound is. Since, according to philosophers, this image is present in the mind itself and we are conscious of it, without doubt it ought to be well known. And yet, as I examine my inner self with the most diligent search, I am unable to discover this image of a sound, nay I am not able even to conceive of its nature. I know of nothing similar to a sound except a sound. And so, I am unable to imagine in my mind what this image of a sound is or what sort of thing it is. Whether you call this image of a sound an idea like Plato, an intelligible form like Aristotle or a phantasm, I do not know what these terms signify. If you should say with Hume that the idea of a sound is something not to be otherwise distinguished from a sound except that it is more weak and feeble, this would have to be nonsense; for who does not know that he can think about a sound when he perceives not even the slightest noise?

If someone should say that by the idea of a sound philosophers mean simply the memory of a sound or the action of the mind when it recalls a sound, I could well understand this, and I confess that I am conscious of this activity. But if they are only signifying this by the phrase, the idea of a sound, to what advantage, I ask, have they expressed something by means of so many terms that are difficult and hard to grasp when they could express it more aptly by well-known ordinary terms? Certainly, it is not fitting for the philosopher to render obscure with words and difficult a thing that is easy and suited to the understanding of the common man. And so, if the idea of anything were to indicate nothing other than the action of the mind in thinking about that thing, whether this action is memory, perception, or imagination, it would have been greatly desired that philosophers define it in this way; nay rather, it would have been more desired that they had never used the terms ideas, phantasms, images, forms, and others similar to these but have been content to employ common idiom when they spoke about things known and familiar to everyone.

But in fact, philosophers do not use the term idea with this meaning, since on this point all agree, namely, that an idea is not an activity of the mind but an object. An idea is not thought itself but a thing about which we think immediately. Such ideas, however, I cannot find in my mind, nay more, I cannot even conceive of them.

It seems no less difficult to me to conceive of the use of ideas than to conceive of their nature. Philosophers state that ideas are the immediate object of thought.[15] Therefore, what the common person calls an object is more remote and mediate; the idea of it is the nearest and the immediate object of thought. And so, the idea of a sound, which I mentioned, is the nearest object; the sound itself is the more remote object. I confess that I do not in any way understand this distinction. All thought must also be reflection about some thing. Moreover, whatever thing we think about, is called the object or material of thought. Since these two points are true, every object of thought seems to me to be equally an immediate object. Nor can I understand what need there is of an intermediate object for thought about something to be possible. I certainly do not deny that of the things observed by the mind, there are different connections, similarities, and bonds, and that the intellect is carried by a certain natural impulse from some one object of reflection to others akin to or connect with it. Thus, from the keen-sighted[1*] Galileo, the mind easily passes to the satellites of Jupiter, first discovered by him. Here, in truth, as soon as the mind has transferred from the astronomer to reflection about the heavenly bodies, these bodies are no less the immediate object of thought than the astronomer was before. Every object of the mind, therefore, appears to be immediate, and although there is a nexus and order of those things that enter the mind, we think about all immediately in their own order; for what it is to think by means of an intermediate object goes completely over my head.

It is probably that in this case (as often happens) philosophers have too rashly applied what happens in the motion of bodies to the reflections of the mind.[16] For it is known to all that a moving force can either be applied immediately to the body to be moved or communicated through intermediary bodies, but no manner of reasoning will persuade that the same process takes place in thought, and that this power of the mind can be applied to an object by the invention of an intermediate object.

If in turn, you ask by which argument philosophers have been led to affirm with such unanimous agreement that ideas exist in the mind as the intermediate objects of perception and memory, I will discuss this argument inasmuch as I have been able to grasp it by examining their works. They say that the human spirit just like every other entity can only exist in that place where it is and when it is. Whether, therefore, you say that perception is the action of the perceived thing on the mind or of the mind on the perceived thing, it is necessary that the mind and the object be together

15. See H 279a; H 224.
1*. Reid calls Galileo, Linceus. This is a reference to Lynceus, the most keen-sighted of the Argonauts. See *The Oxford Classical Dictionary*, s.v. Lynceus.
16. Cf. Berkeley, *Principles of Human Knowledge*, sec. 144; H 237b; H 369.

both in time and place in order that the object can be perceived immediately, since otherwise they cannot mutually affect each other. If, however, the object is external or has passed away, there must be some intermediate body present to and joined with the mind that we call an idea and that can affect the mind immediately.

The whole structure of ideas, therefore, rests on this principle, just like on a foundation, namely, that perception and memory are the actions of the mind on objects or the actions of an object on the mind that require a certain conjunction and contact between mind and object. About this principle two observations must be briefly made.

First of all, the term action is ambiguous and is applied to things of an entirely different type. One speaks of the actions of bodies upon bodies, when they mutually attract, press or strike one another. In these actions of bodies, it is commonly believed that there must be contact or an intermediate body, whether this belief is right or wrong I am not now examining. Furthermore, actions of the mind are said to exist when some object is perceived or remembered, loved or hated, but actions of the mind have nothing in common with the actions of bodies except their name, nor has it been established by any argument that in these actions contact between the mind and the object is necessary, whether as far as place or as far as time is concerned.

Thus, it is evident that this argument [by which philosophers accept the existence of ideas][2*] is in fact a *petitio principii*, and it owes all of its force to the common prejudice noted above, namely, that we too rashly and without reason wish to apply the characteristics that are proper to bodies to the immaterial mind. From this source arises the practice, which is employed by the masses, of attributing human form to God and the angels. From this prejudice, philosophers, through many ages, have ascribed a fiery or airlike nature to the human soul, and from the same prejudice, also, we believe that the operations of the intellect and the actions of bodies are of the same type and subject to the same laws. Nor, in truth, should it seem very surprising that philosophers have for so long reached an agreement about a belief that is based on a prejudice to which the human mind is so prone.

I pass over the fact that in this argument it is set forth that place is characteristic of the immaterial souls no less than of bodies, although, to say the least, this is completely uncertain.

Second, this argument that is advanced on behalf of the existence of ideas, if it proves anything, it proves too much, for it compels us either

---

2*. I have added the words in the square brackets to elucidate the reference Reid is making.

to recall the intelligible forms of the Peripatetics, derided now by the whole world, or to surrender to the Skeptics and to believe that there is nothing in the nature of things except ideas of which we are now conscious. For if we grant that an external object cannot be perceived without an intermediate object joined or connected to the mind, is it not necessary, I ask, for this intermediate object to be joined also to the object perceived? Without doubt, this is necessary, for in no other way can the mind affect the object, or the object the mind.

In no way can the mind and an external object act upon each other mutually, unless an intermediate object is joined to the extremity of each, and it transfers or extends itself from one to the other without any gap. Ideas lie concéaled in the mind, nor do they touch an object. Just as a ship cannot be held by the biting tooth of the anchor when the rope is not attached to the anchor but lies coiled in the interior of the ship, in the same way it does not seem less absurd to suppose that the mind can affect an object or be affected by it by means of an idea that is in the mind but that does not touch the object. This point appears to have been fully grasped by Aristotle who for this reason taught that ideas or forms were sent forth from the object.

And so the doctrine of ideas without intelligible forms is not only an hypothesis but an hypothesis mutilated and unsuitable for solving the problem. Furthermore, I say that with these intelligible forms rejected, the doctrine of ideas plunges everything into the abyss of skepticism. For according to this hypothesis, the ideas present in the mind are not merely the immediate but the only object of the intellect. For when the chain that links ideas and things has been broken, all objects that have passed away, all external objects, vanish just like the dreams of a sick man. The ideas of the instant moment are everything; about other things of whatever kind nothing will be known nor will knowledge nor even probable opinion be left in the human mind.

Although, in truth (in my opinion), this is the true and inevitable consequence of the doctrine of ideas as it is handed down by Descartes and modern philosophers, nonetheless, it would be completely unfair to accuse either Descartes himself or Malebranche or Locke who are supporters of this system of being skeptics. The bond of religion, the love of the human race, and the force of common sense have held these prudent men in check, nor have they allowed either these philosophers or others to sink down into the pit of skepticism. Berkeley, to be sure, perceived that the existence of the material world could not concur with the existence of ideas and he demonstrated this point most lucidly. And, therefore, he dismissed the material world that he thought could be rejected without loss to, nay rather with great advantage for, religion. As far as his other teachings are concerned, he entrusted himself to the common sense of men, although his own doctrine of ideas struggled against it. For he recognized that he had no idea in his mind of the human mind, of other spiritual beings, and of the Supreme Power, and yet he knew for certain that these existed. But if we can reason without ideas about the existence of the Supreme Power and the other spiritual beings, why can we not reason as well about other things? I would wish that this most outstanding man had taught us this, for I fear that in this subject he was scarcely consistent.[17]

Finally Hume, who was praised earlier in my speech, was the first to carry through the doctrine of ideas to its final state and he boldly embraced it, packed full with all its consequences and piled up with the dowry of the most abandoned skepticism. And so, this doctrine, adorned with the supreme force of his genius and acuteness, in keeping with his humanity, he entrusted to the human race in his *Treatise of Human Nature* and in his philosophical essays. The system of Hume is aptly and sufficiently consistent, but it leans with its whole weight on the hypothesis of ideas, so that if this is removed, the whole instantly collapses; his system is an arrogant bulwark of the skepticism of today.[18]

17. See Berkeley, *Principles of Human Knowledge*, sec. 140; also H 289a.
18. Cf. H 103b.

Oration IV[1]

1762

IT IS THREE YEARS SINCE I UNDERTOOK TO SET FORTH FROM THIS CHAIR certain observations about the human intellect and to entrust them to the judgment of my learned audience. It is now my intention to labor on the same argument once again and to pursue it further.

On the threshold, however, I must frankly confess and also regret that the intellect whose force and acuteness comprise a unique instrument for tracking down the truth and leading it forth from the darkness has itself been covered and enveloped by a thick gloom that the keenness of the human mind can scarcely penetrate. I regret also that there is no section of philosophy in the explanation of which more time and labor have been wasted by philosophers both ancient and modern.

Just as the eye looking forth in every direction does not see itself, so the intellect, attentive to and occupied with external objects, escapes notice of itself. The intellect scarcely ever, or not without supreme effort and difficulty, turns its keen vision to itself and its own operations.[2]

For this reason without doubt, it happens that although several sections of philosophy, namely, astronomy, mechanics, hydrostatics, optics, and chemistry, have been built on a solid foundation and daily receive increases worthy of the human mind and no longer cause ambiguity to exist among the learned about their first principles, yet the views of philosophers about perception, judgment, and ideas are almost all obscure, doubtful, entangled with knotty subtleties, paradoxical, in strong opposition to the common sense of men, and favorable to the acatalepsy of the Skeptics.

For this reason also, it has happened that prudent men of sound mind have despised questions and disputes about those subjects that depend on the fabric of the human intellect and that are commonly termed metaphysics, neither expecting fruit from these disputes nor hoping for a solution

1. Most of the topics in this Oration have already been cross-referenced in the footnotes to Oration III.
2. Cf. H 98.

of them. Nay also, warned by the example of the men of the most keen genius, they fear that a more subtle examination of these questions will lead them into the camp of the Skeptics.

From these indications a serious suspicion arises that the views of philosophers about ideas, perception, and judgment, although admitted by common agreement, should not be rashly accepted. For this reason, I have desired for a long time to subject these views once again to an accurate examination lest anything false or ambiguous lies concealed within them that could oppose the truth and, just like a will-o'-the-wisp, be able to lead us aside into the barren and gloomy wilderness of skepticism.

It is right for one who is entering this camp and offering new views on a subject difficult and obscure to ask the indulgence and good faith of his learned audience in case, as often happens, I shall seem to have failed in an undertaking that was honorable and worthy of a philosopher. And if in treating this scholastic subject I am compelled to use scholastic words and language, I hope that my fair-minded audience will grant me pardon in such a subject.

It is sufficiently known that those who have written on the intellect have decided there are three operations of the mind. The first of these is simple apprehension, which is expressed by a term either simple or compound. Moreover, they mean by term some part of a proposition, whether the subject or the predicate. The second operation of the intellect is called judgment, that is, opinion or belief, which is signified by a proposition that affirms or denies. The third operation is reflection or reasoning, which is expressed by a syllogism or a series of propositions. Furthermore, they teach that there are three types of simple apprehension, namely, sensation, imagination, and pure intellect; they attribute to sensation and imagination images of corporeal things in the brain.

It is evident that right from the age of Plato all philosophers have agreed that the intellect does not perceive things that are external or have passed away immediately or by itself, but by means of intermediate ideas, species, forms, or phantasms in the mind or in the brain that are the equivalent of things. They believe that these ideas in every act of perception, in every mediation, and in discourse are the immediate object of the intellect, and that the intellect is empty by nature and incapable of every operation until it is equipped with the ideas, the subject matter, as it were, of thought, which the mind receives either from the senses or from reflection about its own operation. They think that the mind stores the ideas, whether of sensation or reflection, in the memory and later arranges, divides, and compares them, and that judgments are formed by a certain agreement or disagreement perceived among the ideas.

It is sufficient to touch on these views of philosophers briefly and piece-meal, since they are known to everyone. Most of these in truth seem to be fictitious and scarcely in accord with nature.

This is true first of all because these philosophers confine simple apprehension in such narrow limits and say it is defined by terms only but not by propositions. For although judgment is never expressed by a term but by a proposition, nothing prevents simple apprehension from being expressed by either a term or a proposition or even a series of propositions. For who, even from the common masses, would be so dull as to fail to perceive that it is one thing to understand a proposition or a speech, that is to apprehend it simply, and another thing to give an opinion whether it is true or false? From these points, it is established that terms are to be ascribed to apprehension only, but propositions to both apprehension and judgment. Nay more, a judgment never results from a proposition that is not joined to the apprehension of the proposition.

Secondly [these view of philosophers are fictitious],[1*] because they teach that in sensation and imagination there are images in the brain or in the *sensorium*. In what way, I ask, have they made this discovery? Who has ever found images of things in a dissected brain? Who has ever demonstrated either by a definite indication or even a probable argument that images are present in the brain? These views, therefore, are fictitious and in no way firmly fixed, and for this reason they are unworthy of philosophers.

We know, to be sure, that there are images of visible objects in the fund of the eye, and we can show by which law they are formed by the refraction of the rays of light. That these images, however, are not perceived by the mind and are not the immediate object of the intellect is established even from this fact, that in the disease called *Amaurosis* or *Gutta Serena* images are sufficiently distinct in the fund of the eye but are not, however, seen by the mind. This point is made clear from the following fact as well, that there are two images of any object seen by the eyes, one in each eye, but the mind sees not two images but one thing.

Nor is it probable that these images penetrate into the brain, since it is opaque and impervious to the rays of light.

Certainly, we do not deny that the rays of light in some manner affect the membrane of the retina, the choroid, and the optic nerve that is joined to these, but this happens in a way equally unknown to philosophers and to laymen.

1*. I have added the words in the square brackets to fill in the ellipsis Reid is making.

Nor do we deny that this effect on the optic nerve, of whatever type it is, is linked with the perception of the mind, which we call vision, by a binding law of nature or by the will of God who is mightiest and best. Thus far, we advance safely with experience as our guide, nor is it the human lot to penetrate further into these secrets of nature. As far as the other senses are concerned, there is not even the slightest indication that the images of perceived things are formed either in the sensory organs or in the brain.

Images, therefore, in the brain or sensorium, whether they are employed in sensation or imagination, are a figment of the human mind. This figment is sufficiently suited perhaps to poetic or rhetorical adornment but is in truth completely useless for philosophical reasoning, and we leave it to those who have dreamed on Parnassus with its double peaks.

Closely akin to these images are the views of all the philosophers about ideas, since they assert that apprehension takes place by the use of ideas or species existing in the mind that represent things to us and are their equivalent and that are the immediate object of the intellect in all thought.

Plato proposed that there were ideas of all things, which were eternal and unchangeable, and that all knowledge was dependent on these; he believed that the Supreme Mind, when it founded and built this world, gazed upon these ideas as though upon a model.

Aristotle often refuted the opinion of Plato about eternal ideas. Nevertheless, he himself taught that forms of all things, both sensible and intelligible, flew, as it were, from things and were imprinted on the intellect and were the instruments of sensation and intelligence. Lucretius teaches that the Epicurean school was of almost the same opinion, for in the fourth book of the *De Rerum Natura*, he sings persuasively while philosophizing in the worst fashion, as follows:

Come now, hear what bodies stir the mind and learn from a few statements whence arise the bodies which enter the mind. First of all I tell you this, that many images of things wander in many ways, on all sides, and in all directions, of a thin structure, which easily unite in the air when they meet, just like spider's web or leaf of gold. In truth these images are much thinner in texture than the images which strike the eyes and stimulate the vision, since these penetrate through the spaces in the body and stir up the thin nature of the mind within and provoke sensation. And thus we see Centaurs, the limbs of Scyllas, the faces of dogs like Cerberus, and images of those for whom death is over and whose bones the earth embraces. For images of every kind are being carried about everywhere, some which arise spontaneously in the air itself, some which come off of various objects, others which are made from a combination of these shapes. For certainly no image of a Centaur arises from one living, since there has never been a living creature with such a nature. When, however, the images of a man and a horse meet by chance, they easily adhere immediately, as I have said before, because of their subtle nature and fine texture. All other images of this type are created in the same way. When these images are carried about with mobility because of their extreme lightness, as I have shown before, any one of these subtle images easily affects our mind with one blow, for the mind is thin and is in itself wonderfully easy to move.[2*]

This belief about species flying from things and wandering images is seen to have flourished right up to the time of Descartes. Under his guidance and teaching, modern philosophers have rejected the view that intelligible forms are sent forth from things. Nonetheless, they believe that ideas or forms must be held in the mind on the grounds that these are necessary for all perception and thought; they have been little worried about the source from which these ideas enter the mind. All the teaching about the operations of the intellect handed down by Descartes, Malebranche, Locke, Berkeley, and Hume depends on ideas. Nay also, the most faithful interpreter of nature, Newton, the glory of his race and age, who has censured, more than anyone, hypotheses in philosophy and, more than anyone, has tried with great diligence to avoid them, has nonetheless slipped unawarely into this hypothesis and has been carried away, as it were, by a favorable current. This question he sets forth modestly in accordance with his custom at the end of his *Optics*. "Is not the Sensory of Animals that place to which the sensitive Substance is present, and into which the sensible Species of Things are carried through the Nerves and Brain, that there they may be perceived by their immediate presence to that Substance? And these things being rightly dispatch'd does it not appear from Phaenomena that there is a Being incorporeal, living, intelligent, omnipresent, who in infinite Space, as it were in his Sensory, sees the things themselves intimately, and thoroughly perceives them, and comprehends them wholly by their immediate presence to himself: Of which things the Images only carried through the Organs of Sense into our little Sensorius, are there seen and beheld by that which in us perceives and thinks."[3]

Since, in truth, in philosophical subjects neither the reverence of antiquity nor the authority of mighty names has as much force as the weight of proofs and arguments, we have dared to dispense freely with this belief about the existence of ideas or images in the mind and we have copiously treated this subject. Nor is there time now to repeat the arguments by which we attempted to show that this opinion is prejudiced and was never proved

2*. Lucretius, *De Rerum Natura* 4.722–48.
3. Newton, *Optics* (New York: Dover, 1952), bk. 3, pt. ques. 28, p. 370.

by philosophers with solid arguments but rather was held as a conceded principle. We attempted to show that it derived its origin from a practice, to which the human mind is very prone, namely, of imagining that the operations of the mind are mutually similar in themselves to the actions of bodies. From this practice also, it has happened that almost all terms in every language that signify the operations of the intellect are taken from bodily activities, as for example, apprehension, comprehension, conception, imagination, and others similar to these.

Hence also, since in corporeal things the "apprehended" object must be contiguous and conjoined to the "apprehending" agent, and the thing "conceived" must be contiguous and conjoined to the "conceiving" agent, we rashly infer that the same thing happens in the operations of the mind, being swept off our feet by customary words and natural prejudice. Philosophers have been led by this same prejudice right up to the time of Descartes to attribute a fiery or airlike nature to the human soul.[4]

Since, in truth, it is evident to one who examines the problem rather carefully that the nature of the mind and body are completely distinct, and that their operations are entirely different, it must not be rashly concluded that such dissimilar entities are subject to the same laws. Nor is it established by any argument that thought about objects that are remote or have passed away does not occur immediately without an idea or an image, acting as a substitute, being imprinted on the mind.

Although the manner in which cognition of things enters the mind escapes us, we must not for that reason fashion hypotheses. It is a fine thing, and one worthy of a philosopher, to confess that he does not know what he does not know rather than to contaminate philosophy with fictitious hypotheses. Not less does the manner in which the mind sees things present to itself or with what eyes it beholds them escape us, although according to this hypothesis the mind would have to be shortsighted, inasmuch as it cannot see objects far removed without the aid of the eye lenses of ideas.

The consequences of the hypothesis are hard to accept and inconsistent with reason. For what is an image of an immaterial thing of which neither form nor figure is characteristic? What is the image of a material thing imprinted on the mind that is incorporeal and without extension? What is the process of thinking about something not immediately but by means of an intermediate object? In what way does it become known to us that ideas play the role not of themselves but of other things and are a model? In what way does one idea represent for us an object that is present, another,

4. Cf. John Austin on "trailing clouds of etymology" in "A Plea for Excuses," *Philosophical Papers* (Oxford, 1961), pp. 149–51.

an object that is near, another, a thing that is far removed, one idea, an object that has passed away, another, a thing that will exist in the future, one idea, an object in existence, another, a figment of the imagination?

Finally, we demonstrated that this hypothesis leads us straight to the acatalepsy of the Skeptics, for with the removal of the communication between mind and objects, ideas now existing in the mind are not merely the immediate but the only object of the intellect. All external things, all things that have passed away, vanish just like the dreams of a sick man. About these things neither knowledge nor even probably opinion remains in the human mind.[5]

Berkeley embraced this consequence of the theory of ideas insofar as the material world is concerned, and he demonstrated it most lucidly. As far as the other features of the theory are concerned, the most clever Hume built on that foundation a most abandoned system of skepticism that rests with its whole weight on the hypothesis of ideas, but if this is removed, the whole structure instantly collapses.

Since, in truth, we have fully treated these arguments against the existence of ideas in the mind before, we will not tarry over them now. What if the question should now arise whether, on these grounds, the term *idea* should be completely rejected by philosophers? I believe that this is hardly necessary, since customary terms are more easily explained when they are used with a transferred meaning. It is easily perceived by one who has read through philosophical writings with an attentive mind that the word 'idea' is extremely ambiguous. For, first of all, to have an idea of a thing sometimes signifies nothing other than the process of thinking about that thing. Second, my idea of anything signifies what I conceive about the nature of the thing, whether it is true or false. And so, perhaps the rustic's idea of the moon is that it is a body which is flat, round, and a yard wide. The astronomer's idea of the moon, however, is that it is a spherical body illuminated by the sun and about equal in size to one-eighth of the earth. Third, the term idea is sometimes attributed to the offspring of the human mind that in fact have never existed. And so, the *Utopia* of More, or the *Oceana* of Harrington, the ideas of forms of government, are called ideas. Nothing prevents the term from being used in this way. If, however, by the term *idea* there is signified the image of something, existing either in the mind or in the brain, which is the immediate object of the intellect when the mind thinks about anything, I believe that ideas in this sense is the fictitious hypothesis of philosophers, favorable to the views of skeptics but an impediment to sane or useful knowledge.[6]

5. Cf. H 109a.
6. Cf. H 224b.

And so, dismissing the doctrine of ideas, I now pass to other views of philosophers about apprehension.

Although philosophers, in truth, believe that apprehension is threefold, comprised of sensation, imagination, and pure intellect, this distinction appears to be entirely inconsistent with the nature of apprehension. For if in imagination there is no image in the brain, a point that I have attempted thus far to demonstrate, the distinction between imagination and pure intellect disappears. If, however, anyone thinks it is absurd for imagination to exist without an image, let him be aware that he is being deceived by the term, and that by this same token he would deduce that the intellect cannot apprehend without a hand nor conceive without a pregnant womb.

Moreover, the nature of sensation itself persuades us that it is not a form of simple apprehension. For in every sensation, the conception is not bare and simple, as in imagination, but joined to assent and belief. While I sit alone at the hearth of my bedchamber, I can fashion in my imagination an assembly of listeners, without adding any assent or judgement, but when from this chair I behold this learned assembly with my eyes, it is impossible for me not to believe it is present and I am overcome with modesty.

The senses are witnesses of perceived objects; we understand their testimony with nature as our interpreter, and we furnish the most firm assent to it with the same nature as our guide. The same statement must also be made about the memory of objects that have passed away. For in this operation of the mind, no less than in sensation, apprehension is not simple but joined with judgment, that is, with belief and assent. And so, we recognize that imagination is the only kind of simple apprehension.

From the following points also, one can learn how little the belief that simple apprehension is the primary operation of the intellect, is in accord with nature. This hypothesis supposes that the mind is first of all equipped with ideas and that afterward, by comparing these ideas, it forms judgments. For since sensation is prior to imagination, it will follow from such statements that apprehension joined with judgment and belief is prior to simple apprehension. Judgments, therefore, are not formed from simple apprehensions by an arrangement of these apprehensions; rather it must be said that simple apprehensions are formed from judgments that are primary and natural by means of analysis or resolution.

About the nature of judgment and its distinction from apprehension, little now remains to be said. For I fear that in this matter what is understood distinctly enough by unlearned men, philosophers have rendered obscure in their attempt to explain and define what cannot be defined. For if you attempt to dissect, reveal, and define what is entirely simple and *sui generis*, your attempt will be in vain; it can oppose the truth but never be of profit to it. If anyone wished to define whiteness and explain how it differs from a dark blue color, will he succeed in any way? Certainly he will render a thing that is obvious to the eyes, obscure by his words. The same will happen if you seek what judgment, opinion, and belief are and how they are distinguished from simple apprehension. Everyone knows their nature full well, taught by the consciousness of these operations. If, however, a man busies himself with definition and explanation, he will conceal in the densest gloom a thing that is perfectly obvious by its own light and he will embrace a cloud in place of Juno.[3*]

It seems in fact that this has happened to two most shrewd philosophers, John Locke and David Hume, in this very subject. Locke asserts that judgment is the perception of the agreement or disagreement of ideas. And on this definition, a great portion of his *An Essay Concerning Human Understanding* and, to be sure, a great part of his teaching about the intellect, which is now commonly accepted, are based. And so, we must weigh this definition rather carefully, since I believe that it errs both in genus and in species.

First of all, let us consider his view in relation to genus. Locke intimates that perception is a genus of which judgment is a species. But what is perception? This certainly is in need of definition no less than, nay more than, judgment. Without doubt it signifies some activity of the intellect. Which activity, however? It is not judgment, since this in itself must be defined. It is not simple apprehension. And so, let us propose the only view that remains, namely, that perception is used here as a general term embracing all operations of the intellect, and thus the definition will arrive at this point: judgment is a certain operation of the intellect about the agreement or disagreement of ideas. By this view, however, judgment is not distinguished from simple apprehension. For it has been demonstrated before that propositions, whether about the agreement of ideas or about some other thing, are to be applied not only to judgment, but also to simple apprehension. So much for the genus of the definition.

As far as the species is concerned, we must ask whether judgment is employed in examining the agreement or disagreement of ideas but in no other matter. If it is only involved in this activity, woe is me, since neither my soul is an idea nor my friends, associates, parents, kinfolk nor my fatherland are ideas, nor are the world and the Founder and most wise Ruler of the world ideas. About these objects, about their existence, attributes, relationships, there will be no judgment, nothing will be established,

---

3*. The reference here is to the legend in Greek mythology about Ixion. He attempted to violate the chastity of Hera (Juno) but was deceived by a cloud image of her. He was later punished for his offense by being attached to a revolving wheel.

nothing discovered, not even probability! But did Locke mean this? God forbid! It would be thoroughly wrong and shameful to attribute such monstrosities of opinions to a man who was truly most outstanding and who has served his fatherland, the human race, and the Christian religion in an excellent fashion. Carried incautiously into the hypothesis of ideas, he set forth principles about the intellect that were in agreement with this hypothesis. But if he had perceived that this hypothesis and the principles of it were fruitful of such terrifying consequences that were contrary to knowledge, virtue, and religion, without doubt this excellent man would have held them in suspicion and weighed them more severely. Since, however, Hume avidly embraces these monsters of opinions, let him delight in them, as far as I am concerned, nor do I envy him. But now I pass to the definition of judgment given by Hume himself.

This most shrewd man asserts boldly in accord with his custom that apprehension and judgment are of the same genus, nor is there any difference between them except that judgment strikes the mind more strongly, apprehension, more weakly. He believes that sensation, memory, belief, and imagination differ only in degree, not in type, in proportion as the ideas are stronger or weaker. Therefore, the man who, in reading a tale of Aesop, is struck strongly by the ideas believes the tale, the man who is struck more weakly, understands the tale but does not believe it. For this philosopher reasons in the following way. Since the man who believes and the man who only understands have the same ideas in their minds, there will be, therefore, no difference between these activities except in the force or weakness of the ideas.

You will observe that this philosophical madness also was born of the same hypothesis of ideas, an offspring worthy of its parent. I wish that this acute philosopher had stated what was the difference between contrary judgments, for these have the same ideas, and the ideas in both will be strong, since they form judgments. It follows, as far as I can see, that contrary judgments are the same not only in type but also in degree.

But, in fact, ravings of this type should be laughed at rather than refuted. And so, in a matter so obvious it is sufficient to observe this point alone, that the intellect in relation to the same object can exercise entirely different operations. Just as the object of love and hate can be the same, and yet it does not follow that hate is a degree of love, so the same proposition can be conceived by the intellect simply or with an opinion expressed about it, whether it is true or false. These operations are of an entirely different type, no less than sound is different from sight. Each person taught by his own consciousness perceives clearly their nature and difference, but since they are simple and *sui genesis* they cannot be defined.

There are other dogmas of philosophers that should be weighed, perhaps on another occasion if God is willing. Not, however, with the intention of disparaging philosophy or philosophers, a purpose that is far from me, do I wish these statements to be understood. I make them in order that, when the empty figments of the human mind have been rejected in this part of philosophy, no less than in physics, whether these arose from ancient or modern philosophers, whether they have been accepted incautiously by lovers of truth and virtue, whether they have been contrived purposely by others, in place of them truer and more useful views can be substituted. It is right to hope that these will be attained if we examine with a mind pure and free from prejudice the human intellect, the supreme work of God, most difficult, to be sure, to understand, but most worthy to be reflected upon.

Bibliography

Books by or about Thomas Reid

Butts, Robert E., and John W. Davis, eds. *The Methodological Heritage of Newton.* Toronto: University of Toronto Press, 1970.

Daniels, Norman. *Thomas Reid's "Inquiry": The Geometry of Visibles and the Case for Realism.* New York: Burt Franklin, 1974.

Davie, George E. *The Democratic Intellect: Scotland and Her Universities in the Nineteenth Century.* Edinburgh: Edinburgh University Press, 1961.

Duncan, Elmer H., ed. *Thomas Reid's Lectures on Natural Theology* (1780). With an essay, "Reid: First Principles and Reason in the Lectures on Natural Theology," by William R. Eakin. Washington, D. C.: University Press of America, 1981.

Ferreira, M. Jamie. *Skepticism and Reasonable Doubt.* Oxford: Clarendon Press, 1986.

Grave, S. A. *The Scottish Philosophy of Common Sense,* Oxford: Clarendon Press, 1960.

Jones, O. Mckendree. *Empiricism and Intuition in Reid's Common Sense Philosophy.* Princeton: Princeton University Press, 1927.

Keuhn, Manfred. *Scottish Common Sense in Germany, 1768–1800.* Kingston and Montreal: McGill-Queen's University Press, 1987.

Marcil-Lacoste, Louise. *Claude Buffier and Thomas Reid: Two Common-Sense Philosophers.* Kingston and Montreal: McGill-Queen's University Press, 1982.

Martin, Terence. *The Instructed Vision: Scottish Common Sense Philosophy and the Origins of American Fiction.* Bloomington: Indiana University Press, 1961.

McCosh, James. *The Scottish Philosophy,* 1875. Reprint. Hildesheim: Georg Olms, 1966.

Olson, Richard. *Scottish Philosophy and British Physics, 1750–1880.* Princeton: Princeton University Press, 1975. Chaps. 1–5 passim.

Reid, Thomas. "A Brief Account of Aristotle's Logic." In *Sketches of the History of Man,* edited by Henry Home, 2:168–241. Glasgow: T. Duncan, 1819.

———. "An Essay on Quantity." *Transactions of the Royal Society of London,* 45:505–20. London, 1748.

———. *Essays on the Active Powers of the Human Mind.* Introduction by Baruch Brody. Cambridge, Mass.: MIT Press, 1969.

———. *Essays on the Intellectual Powers of Man.* Introduction by Baruch Brody. Cambridge, Mass.: MIT Press, 1969.

———. *Essays on the Intellectual Powers of Man.* Edited and abridged by A. D. Woozley. London: Macmillan and Co., 1941.

———. *Inquiry and Essays.* Edited by Keith Lehrer and Ronald E. Beanblossom. Indianapolis: Bobbs-Merrill, 1975.

————. *An Inquiry into the Human Mind, on the Principles of Common Sense.* Introduction by Timothy Duggan. Chicago: University of Chicago Press, 1970.

————. *Lectures on the Fine Arts.* Edited with an introduction by Peter Kivy. International Archives of the History of Ideas Series Minor, no. 7. The Hague: Martinus Nijhoff, 1973.

————. *Philosophical Orations of Thomas Reid.* Edited with an introduction, from the Birkwood manuscript, by W. R. Humphries. Aberdeen: Aberdeen University Press, 1937.

————. *Philosophical Works.* 8th ed. 2 vols. With notes and supplementary dissertations by Sir William Hamilton, and an introduction by Harry M. Bracken. 1895. Reprint. Hildesheim: Georg Olms, 1967.

————. "Unpublished Letters of Thomas Reid to Lord Kames," edited by Ian Ross. *Texas Studies in Literature and Language* (1965): 17–65.

Schneider, Louis, ed. *The Scottish Moralists on Human Nature and Society. Selected papers of Adam Smith, David Hume, Adam Ferguson, Thomas Reid, Francis Hutcheson, Dugald Stewart, Lord Kames, and Lord Monboddo,* Chicago: University of Chicago Press, 1967.

Seth (Pringle-Pattison), Andrew. *Scottish Philosophy.* Edinburgh: William Blackwood and Sons, 1885.

Stewart, Dugald. *Biographical Memoirs of Adam Smith, William Robertson, and of Thomas Reid. Read before the Royal Society of Edinburgh.* Edinburgh, 1811.

Selected Articles on Thomas Reid and Scottish Philosophy

Angell, R. B. "The Geometry of Visibles." *Nous* 8 (1974): 87–117.

Ardley, Gavin. "Hume's Common Sense Critics." *Revue Internationale de Philosophie* 30 (1976): 104–25.

Beanblossom, Ronald E. "In Defense of Thomas Reid's Use of Suggestion." *Grazer Philosophische Studien* 1 (1975): 19–24.

————. "Russell's Indebtedness to Reid." *Monist* 61, 2 (April 1978): 192–204.

Ben-Zeev, Aaron. "Reid's Direct Approach to Perception." *Studies in the History and Philosophy of Science* 25 (Summer 1986).

Bourdillon, Philip. "Thomas Reid's Account of Sensation as a Natural Principle of Belief." *Philosophical Studies* 27 (January 1975): 19–36.

Bracken, Harry. "Thomas Reid: A Philosopher of Un-Common Sense." from the introduction to the *Philosophical Works of Thomas Reid,* edited by Sir William Hamilton. Hildesheim: Georg Olms Verlag, 1967.

Broadie, Alexander. "Medieval Notions And The Theory of Ideas." *Proceedings of the Aristotelian Society* (1987): 153–67.

Brody, Baruch. "Hume, Reid, and Kant on Causality." In *Thomas Reid: Critical Interpretations,* edited by Stephen F. Barker and Tom L. Beauchamp, pp. 8–13. Philadelphia: Temple University Press, 1976.

————. "Reid and Hamilton on Perception." *Monist* 55 (1971): 423–41.

Caldwell, R. L. "Another Look at Thomas Reid." *Journal of the History of Ideas* 23 (1962): 545–49.

Cantor, G. N. "Berkeley, Reid, and the Mathematization of Mid-Eighteenth Century Optics." *Journal of the History of Ideas* 38 (1977): 429–48.

Capaldi, Nicholas. "Reid's Critique of Hume's Moral Theory." *Philosophical Journal* 5 (1968).
Casullo, Albert. "Reid and Mill on Hume's Maxim of Conceivability." *Analysis* 39 (October 1979): 212–19.
Chisholm, Roderick. "Evidence as Justification." *Journal of Philosophy* 58 (1961): 739–48.
———. "Freedom and Action." In *Freedom and Determinism,* edited by Keith Lehrer. New York: Random House, 1966.
Cummins, Phillip D. "Berkeley's Ideas of Sense." *Nous* 9 (1975): 55–72.
———. "Reid on Abstract General Ideas." In *Thomas Reid: Critical Interpretations,* edited by Stephen F. Barker and Tom L. Beauchamp, pp. 62–76. Philadelphia: Temple University Press, 1976.
———. "Reid's Realism." *Journal of the History of Philosophy* 12 (August 1974): 317–40.
Daniels, Norman. "On Having Concepts 'By Our Constitution.' " In *Thomas Reid: Critical Interpretations,* edited by Stephen F. Barker and Tom L. Beauchamp, pp. 103–12. Philadelphia: Temple University Press, 1976.
———. "Thomas Reid's Discovery of a Non-Euclidean Geometry." *Philosophy of Science* 39 (June 1972): 219–34.
Davenport, Alan Wade. "Reid's Indebtedness to Bacon." *Monist* 70, 4 (October 1987): 496–507.
Davie, G. E. "Berkeley's Impact on Scottish Philosophers." *Philosophy* 40 (1965): 222–34.
———. "Hume and the Origins of the Common Sense School." *Revue Internationale de Philosophie* 6 (1952): 213–21.
Davis, Merrell R. "Emerson's 'Reason' and the Scottish Philosophers." *New England Quarterly* 17 (1944): 209–28.
Day, J. P. "Appendix: Kant and Reid on Berkeley's Immaterialism," appended to "George Berkeley, 1685–1753." *Review of Metaphysics* 6 (1953): 591–96.
Duggan, Timothy. "Active Power and the Liberty of Moral Agents." *Thomas Reid: Critical Interpretations,* edited by Stephen F. Barker and Tom L. Beauchamp, pp. 103–12. Philadelphia: Temple University Press, 1976.
———. "Ayer and Reid: Responses to the Skeptic." *Monist* 61, no. 2 (April 1978): 205–19.
———. "Thomas Reid's Theory of Sensation." *Philosophical Revue* 69 (January 1960): 90–100.
Duncan, Elmer H. "Eighteenth-Century Scottish Philosophy: Its Impact on the American West." *Southwestern Journal of Philosophy* 6 (Winter 1975): 131–48.
Duncan, Elmer H., and Robert M. Baird. "Thomas Reid's Criticism of Adam Smith's Theory of the Moral Sentiment." *Journal of the History of Ideas* 38 (1977): 509–22.
Dür, Seweryn. "Reid's Criticism of Hume's Epistemology." *Studia Filozoficzne* 29 (1962).
Ellos, W. J. "Thomas Reid's Analysis of Sensation." *New Scholasticism* 57 (Winter 1983): 107–14.
Faurot, Jean H. "Common Sense in the Philosophy of Thomas Reid." *Modern Schoolman* 33 (1956): 182–89.
———. "The Development of Reid's Theory of Knowledge." *University of Toronto Quarterly* 21, no. 3 (1952): 224–31.

———. "Reid's Reply to Joseph Priestley." *Journal of the History of Ideas* 39 (1978): 285–92.

———. "Thomas Reid, on Intelligible Objects." *Monist* 61, no. 2 (April 1978): 229–44.

Gallie, Roger. "The Same Self." *Locke Newsletter* 18 (1987): 45–62.

Gracyk, Theodore A. "The Failure of Thomas Reid's Aesthetics." *Monist* 70, no. 4 (October 1987): 465–82.

Grave, S. A. "Common Sense." In *Encyclopedia of Philosophy,* edited by Paul Edwards. New York: Macmillan Co., 1967.

———. "The 'Theory of Ideas.' " *Thomas Reid: Critical Interpretations,* edited by Stephen F. Barker and Tom L. Beauchamp, 55–61. Philadelphia: Temple University Press, 1976.

———. "Thomas Reid." In *Encyclopedia of Philosophy,* edited by Paul Edwards. New York: Macmillan Co., 1967.

Greenberg, Arthur R. "Hamilton and Reid's Realism." *Modern Schoolman* 54 (1976): 15–32.

———. "Reid, Berkeley, and Notional Knowledge." *Monist* 61, no. 2 (April 1978): 271–82.

———. "Reid on Primary and Secondary Qualities." *New Essays on Rationalism and Empiricism. Canadian Journal of Philosophy,* supp. 4 (1977): 207–18.

Hanick, James G. "Thomas Reid and Common Sense Foundationalism." *New Scholasticism* 60, no. 1 (Winter 1986): 91–115.

Hazelton, W. Dean. "On an Alleged Inconsistency in Reid's Theory of Moral Liberty." *Journal of the History of Philosophy* 16 (October 1978): 453–55.

Heath, Peter. "Reid on Conceiving and Imagining." *Monist* 61, no. 2 (April 1978): 220–28.

Henderson, G. P. "Review of Norman Daniels' *Thomas Reid's Inquiry." Philosophical Books* 17 (1976).

Hooker, Michael, "A Mistake Concerning Conception." In *Thomas Reid: Critical Interpretations,* edited by Stephen F. Barker and Tom L. Beauchamp, pp. 86–94. Philadelphia: Temple University Press, 1976.

Immerwahr, John. "The Development of Reid's Realism." *Monist* 61, no. 2 (April 1978): 245–56.

Jacques, J. H. "The Appeal to Common Sense." *Listener* 43 (1960): 246–52.

Jensen, Henning. "Common Sense and Common Language in Thomas Reid's Ethical Theory." *Monist* 61, no. 2 (April 1978): 299–310.

———. "Reid and Wittgenstein on Philosophy and Language." *Philosophical Studies* 36 (November 1979): 359–76.

Kallich, Martin. "The Argument against the Association of Ideas in Eighteenth-Century Aesthetics." *Modern Language Quarterly* 15 (1954): 125–36.

Kivy, Peter. "The Logic of Taste: Reid and the Second Fifty Years." In *Thomas Reid: Critical Interpretations,* edited by Stephen F. Barker and Tom L. Beauchamp, pp. 113–24. Philadelphia: Temple University Press, 1976.

———. "Reid's Unpublished Lectures on the Fine Arts." *Journal of the History of Ideas* 31, no. 1 (January–March 1970): 17–32.

———. "Thomas Reid and the Expression Theory of Art." *Monist* 61, No. 2, (April 1978): 167–83.

Krolikowski, Walter P. "The Starting Point in Scottish Common-Sense Realism." *Modern Schoolman* 33 (1956): 139–52.

Kuehn, Manfred. "The Early Reception of Reid, Oswald, and Beattie in Germany, 1768–1800." *Journal of the History of Philosophy* 21 (October 1983): 479–96.

Laird, J. Review of Reid's *Essays on the Intellectual Powers of Man,* edited and abridged by A. D. Woozley. *Philosophy* 17 (1942): 89–90.

Laudan, L. L. "Thomas Reid and the Newtonian Turn of British Methodological Thought." In *The Methodological Heritage of Newton,* edited by Robert E. Butts, and John W. Davis, pp. 103–31. Toronto: University of Toronto Press, 1970.

Lehrer, Keith "Beyond Impressions and Ideas: Hume vs. Reid." *Monist* 70, no. 4 (October 1987): 383–97.

———. "Can We Know That We Have Free Will by Introspection?" *Journal of Philosophy* 57 (1960): 145–57.

———. "Reid's Influence on Contemporary American and British Philosophy." In *Thomas Reid: Critical Interpretations,* edited by Stephen F. Barker and Tom L. Beauchamp, pp. 1–7. Philadelphia: Temple University Press, 1976.

———. "Reid on Primary and Secondary Qualities." *Monist* 61, no. 2 (April 1978): 184–91.

———. "Scottish Influences on Contemporary American Philosophy." *Philosophical Journal* 5 (1968).

———. "Why Not Scepticism?" *Philosophical Forum* 11 (1971): 283–98.

Lesser, Harry. "Reid's Criticism of Hume's Theory of Personal Identity." *Hume Studies* 4 (November 1978): 41–63.

Madden, E. H. "Commonsense and Agency Theory." *Review of Metaphysics,* 36 (December 1982): 319–42.

———. "Did Reid's Metaphilosophy Survive Kant, Hamilton and Mill?" *Metaphilosophy* (January 1987): 31–48.

———. "The Metaphilosophy of Common Sense." *American Philosophical Quarterly* 20 (January 1983): 23–36.

———. "Was Reid a Natural Realist?" *Philosophy and Phenomenological Research* 47 (December 1986): 255–76.

Madden, E. H., and J. W. Manns. "Theodore Jouffroy's Contributions to the Common Sense Tradition." *Journal of the History of Philosophy* 24, no. 4 (October 1987): 573–84.

Marcil-Lacoste, Louise. "The Seriousness of Reid's Sceptical Admissions." *Monist* 61, no. 2 (April 1978): 311–25.

McGregor, Joan. "Reid on Justice as a Natural Virtue." *Monist* 70, no. 4 (October 1987): 483–95.

Michael, Fred S., and Michael, Emily. "Reid's Hume: Remarks on Hume in Some Early Logic Lectures of Reid." *Monist* 70, no. 4 (October 1987): 508–26.

Nadler, Steven M. "Reid, Arnauld and the Objects of Perception." *History of Philosophy Quarterly* 3, no. 2 (April 1986): 165–74.

Norton, David Fate. "George Turnbull and the Furniture of the Mind." *Journal of the History of Ideas* 35 (1975): 701–16.

———. "Reid's Abstract of the *Inquiry into the Human Mind.*" In *Thomas Reid: Critical Interpretations,* edited by Stephen F. Barker and Tom L. Beauchamp, pp. 125–32. Philadelphia: Temple University Press, 1976.

Norton, David Fate, and J. C. Stewart-Robertson. "Thomas Reid on Adam Smith's Theory of Morals." *Journal of the History of Ideas* 41 (July–September 1980): 381–98.

Olsen, R. "Scottish Philosophy of Mathematics, 1750–1830." *Journal of the History of Ideas* 32 (1971): 29–44.

Pappas, George S. "Common Sense in Berkeley and Reid." *Revue Internationale de Philosophie* 40 (1986): 292–303.

Peach, Bernard. "Common Sense and Practical Reason in Reid and Kant." *Sophia* 24 (1956): 66–71.

Peirce, C. S. "Issues of Pragmatism." *Monist* 15–16 (1905–6).

Popkin, Richard. "Scepticism." In *Encyclopedia of Philosophy,* edited by Paul Edwards. New York: Macmillan Co., 1967.

Pritchard, Michael S. "Reason and Passion: Reid's Reply to Hume." *Monist* 61, no. 2 (April 1978): 283–98.

Robbins, David O. "The Aesthetics of Thomas Reid." *Journal of Aesthetics and Art Criticism* 5 (1943): 30–41.

Robertson, J. Charles. "Review of Kivy's 'Lectures on the Fine Arts' the Unpublished Manuscripts of Thomas Reid." *Dialogue* 14 (1975): 710–14.

Robinson, Daniel N. "Thomas Reid's *Gestalt* Psychology." In *Thomas Reid: Critical Interpretations,* edited by Stephen F. Barker and Tom L. Beauchamp, pp. 44–54. Philadelphia: Temple University Press, 1976.

Robinson, Daniel N., and Tom L. Beauchamp. "Personal Identity: Reid's Answer to Hume." *Monist* 61, no. 2 (April 1978): 326–39.

Robinson, Wade L. "Hume's Ontological Commitments." *Philosophical Quarterly* 26 (1976): 39–47.

Rollin, Bernard E. "Thomas Reid and the Semiotics of Perception." *Monist* 61, no. 2 (April 1978): 257–70.

Rome, S. C. "The Scottish Refutation of Berkeley's Immaterialism." *Philosophy and Phenomenological Research* 3 (1942–43): 313–25.

Rowe, William L. "Two Concepts of Freedom." *Proceedings of the American Philosophical Association,* supp. 61 (1987): 43–64.

———. "Reid's Conception of Human Freedom." *Monist* 70, no. 4 (October 1987): 430–41.

Seth, James. "Scottish Moral Philosophy." *Philosophical Review* 7 (1900): 561–82.

Silver, Bruce. "A Note on Berkeley's *New Theory of Vision* and Thomas Reid's Distinction between Primary and Secondary Qualities." *Southern Journal of Philosophy* 12 (Summer 1974): 253–63.

Sleigh, Robert C. "Reid and the Ideal Theory of Conception and Perception." In *Thomas Reid: Critical Interpretations,* edited by Stephen F. Barker and Tom L. Beauchamp, pp. 77–85. Philadelphia: Temple University Press, 1976.

Somerville, James. "Reid's Conception of Common Sense." *Monist* 70, no. 4 (October 1987): 418–29.

Stecker, Robert "Thomas Reid on the Moral Sense." *Monist* 70, no. 4 (October 1987): 453–64.

Stephen, Leslie. "Reid." In *The Dictionary of National Biography,* edited by Sir Leslie Stephen and Sidney Lee. Oxford: Oxford University Press, 1921–22.

Stewart-Robertson, J. C. "The Well-Principled Savage, or The Child of the Scottish Enlightenment." *Journal of the History of Ideas* 42 (July–September 1981): 503–25.

Stewart-Robertson, J. C., and D. F. Norton. "Thomas Reid on Adam Smith's Theory of Morals." Pt. 2. *Journal of the History of Ideas* 45 (April–June, 1984): 309–22.

Taylor, Richard. Review of S. A. Grave's *The Scottish Philosophy of Common Sense*. *Philosophical Review* 70 (July 1961): 413–16.

Tebaldi, David A. "Thomas Reid's Refutation of the Argument from Illusion." In *Thomas Reid: Critical Interpretation,* edited by Stephen F. Barker and Tom L. Beauchamp, pp. 25–34. Philadelphia: Temple University Press, 1976.

Thompson, N. W. "Aristotle as a Predecessor to Reid's Common Sense." *Speech Monographs* 42, no. 3 (1975): 209–20.

Todd, D. D. "Reid Redivivus?" *Texas Studies in Literature and Language* 14, no. 2 (Summer 1972): 303–12.

————. Review of Thomas Reid's *Essays on the Active Powers of the Human Mind,* edited by Baruch Brody. *Australasian Journal of Philosophy* 48 (1970): 282–83.

————. Review of Thomas Reid's *Essays on the Intellectual Powers of Man,* edited by Baruch Brody. *Australasian Journal of Philosophy* 48 (1970): 280–82.

————. Review of Thomas Reid's *Lectures on the Fine Arts,* by Peter Kivy. *Journal of the History of Philosophy* 13 (1975): 534–35.

Tsugawa, Albert. "Hume and Kames on Personal Identity." *Journal of the History of Ideas* 22 (1961): 398–403.

Vernier, Paul. "Thomas Reid on the Foundations of Knowledge and His Answer to Skepticism." In *Thomas Reid: Critical Interpretations,* edited by Stephen F. Barker and Tom L. Beauchamp, pp. 14–24. Philadelphia: Temple University Press, 1976.

Weinstock, Jerome A. "Reid's Definition of Freedom." *Journal of the History of Philosophy* 13 (July 1975): 335–45.

————. "Reid's Definition of Freedom." In *Thomas Reid: Critical Interpretations,* edited by Stephen F. Barker and Tom L. Beauchamp, pp. 95–102. Philadelphia: Temple University Press, 1976.

Weldon, Susan. "Direct Realism and Visual Distortion: A Development of Arguments from Thomas Reid." *Journal of the History of Philosophy* 20 (October 1982): 355–68.

Winch, P. G. "The Notion of 'Suggestion' in Thomas Reid's Theory of Perception." *Philosophical Quarterly* 3 (1953): 327–41.

Wolterstorff, Nicholas. "Hume and Reid." *Monist* 70, no. 4 (October 1987): 398–418.

Wood, P. B. "David Hume On Thomas Reid's *An Inquiry into the Human Mind, on the Principles of Common Sense:* A New Letter to Hugh Blaire from July 1762." *Mind* 95 (October 1986): 411–16.

Woozley, A. D. "Reid on Moral Liberty." *Monist* 70, no. 4 (October 1987): 442–52.

Wright, John. "Hume Versus Reid On Ideas: The New Hume Letter." *Mind* 96 (July 1987): 392–98.

Yolton, John W. "Ideas and Knowledge in Seventeenth-Century Philosophy." *Journal of the History of Philosophy* 13 (April 1975): 145–65.

Doctoral Dissertations

Alexander, Henry Aaron. "Thomas Reid's Defense of Common Sense." University of California, 1954.

Beanblossom, Ronald E. "The Use of Metaphor and Analogy in Thomas Reid's Epistemology." University of Rochester, 1970.

Berval, Juan Erminio. "David Hume and Thomas Reid on Objective Existence." University of California, Irvine, 1979.

Bourdillon, Philip. "Berkeley and Reid: An Analysis of Reid's Reaction to Berkeley's Rejection of Material Substance." University of Rochester, 1972.

Caldwell, R. L. "Reid and Hamilton on Perception." University of Washington, 1958.

Castagnetto, Susan Victoria. "Locke and Reid on Abstraction." Stanford University, 1986.

Crombie, E. James. "Thomas Reid's Theory of Immediate Perception." University of Waterloo, 1979.

Daniels, Norman. "Thomas Reid's Discovery of a Non-Euclidean Geometry: A Case Study in the Relation Between Theory and Practice." Harvard University, 1970.

Duggan, Timothy. "Thomas Reid's Theory of Empirical Evidence." Brown University, 1957.

Evans, Meredydd. *Perception and Common Sense in the Writings of Thomas Reid.* Microfilm Publication, No. 13, 690, Princeton University, 1955.

Greenberg, Arthur Richard. "Reid on Scepticism, Idealism, and Perceptual Knowledge." University of Iowa, 1973.

Immerwahr, John R. "Thomas Reid's Theory of Perception." University of Michigan, 1972.

Lamb, Roger E. "Two Epistemological Dogmatists: Reid and Moore." University of Rochester, 1955.

Marshall, Donald K. "The Restoration of Logic in Thomas Reid." University of Chicago, 1939.

Norton, David Fate. "From Moral Sense to Common Sense: An Essay on the Development of Scottish Common Sense Philosophy 1700–1765." University of California, 1966.

Olin, Doris. "Thomas Reid's Theory of Sensation and Perception." Cornell University, 1971.

Peterson, R. "Scottish Common Sense in America 1768–1850, an Evaluation of Its Influence." University of Michigan, 1972.

Powell, Francis De Sales. "A Thomistic evaluation of James Wilson and Thomas Reid." Georgetown University, 1951.

Ratowsky, Henry Allen. "The Theory of Ideas in the Philosophy of Hume and Reid." City University of New York, 1976.

Schwarz, Stephan Dietrich. "Reid and the Justification of Perception." Harvard University, 1966.

Sleigh, Robert Collins. "An Examination of Thomas Reid's Account of Our Knowledge of the External World." Brown University, 1963.

Steinberg, Eric Matthew. "Hume's Attitude Toward Common Sense." Columbia University, 1974.

Tebaldi, David. "Thomas Reid's Refutation of the 'Way of Ideas.' " Rutgers University, 1974.

Vernier, Paul. "Skepticism and Perceptual Belief in the Philosophy of Thomas Reid." John Hopkins University, 1977.

Weldon, Susan. "Thomas Reid's Theory of Vision." McGill University, 1978.

D. D. TODD IS ASSOCIATE PROFESSOR OF PHILOSOPHY IN THE DEPARTment of Philosophy at Simon Fraser University in British Columbia, Canada. He was born in Arkansas and was educated chiefly in California (San Francisco State College, University of California, Berkeley) and Canada (University of British Columbia, Vancouver School of Art). His main publications have been in the area of epistemology, but his strongest current interest is in aesthetics.